Outsiders on the Inside

Outsiders on the Inside

Understanding Racial Fatigue, Racial Resilience, and Racial Hospitality in Our Churches

WILLIAM E. BOYCE

Foreword by Carl F. Ellis, Jr.

WIPF & STOCK · Eugene, Oregon

OUTSIDERS ON THE INSIDE
Understanding Racial Fatigue, Racial Resilience, and Racial Hospitality in Our Churches

Copyright © 2022 William E. Boyce. All rights reserved. Except for brief quotations in critical publications or reviews, no part of this book may be reproduced in any manner without prior written permission from the publisher. Write: Permissions, Wipf and Stock Publishers, 199 W. 8th Ave., Suite 3, Eugene, OR 97401.

Wipf & Stock
An Imprint of Wipf and Stock Publishers
199 W. 8th Ave., Suite 3
Eugene, OR 97401

www.wipfandstock.com

PAPERBACK ISBN: 978-1-6667-1938-3
HARDCOVER ISBN: 978-1-6667-1939-0
EBOOK ISBN: 978-1-6667-1940-6

04/06/22

Unless otherwise indicated, Scripture quotations are from the ESV® Bible (The Holy Bible, English Standard Version®), Copyright © 2001 by Crossway, a publishing ministry of Good News Publishers. Used by permission. All rights reserved.

Quotations of the New International Version, THE HOLY BIBLE, NEW INTERNATIONAL VERSION®, NIV® Copyright © 1973, 1978, 1984, 2011 by Biblica, Inc.™ Used by permission. All rights reserved worldwide.

A previous version of chapter 3 appeared as "A Doctrine for Diversity: Utilizing Herman Bavinck's Theology for Racial Reconciliation in the church," in *Journal of Markets and Morality*, 23.2, Fall 2020. Used with permission.

To Mrs. Mary Rankin,
who instilled a passion for racial justice into the second-grade class at Madison Elementary School, teaching us always to keep our "eyes on the prize" with grace, dignity, and love.

And to the twelve pastors who entrusted me with their stories in this book, with admiration and gratitude for your witness, your ministry, and your friendship. Thank you for keeping your "eyes on the prize" of our faith (Phil 3:13–14).

Contents

List of Tables and Figures ... ix
Foreword by Carl F. Ellis, Jr. ... xi
Introduction ... xv
Key Terms and Concepts ... xxiii

PART I | RACIAL HOSPITALITY IN SCRIPTURE AND TRADITION

1. All Races Welcome? ... 3
2. Outsiders in the Kingdom? ... 24
   Racial Inclusivity and Biblical Theology
3. Why Diversity? ... 47
   A Reformed Theology of Church Diversity

PART II | RACIAL HOSPITALITY IN THE PCA

4. Charting the Minority Experience: ... 65
   Toward a Phenomenology of Black PCA Pastors
5. Welcome to the PCA! ... 70
6. Outsiders on the Inside ... 74
7. Learning to Thrive ... 101
8. Conclusions ... 121

Acknowledgments ... 137
Bibliography ... 139

List of Tables and Figures

Figure 1: Original Creation: Ordered and Bounded (Genesis 1)	26
Figure 2: Post-Fall Humanity Divided (Genesis 3)	28
Figure 3: Insiders and Outsiders in the Old Testament	34
Figure 4: Insiders and Outsiders in the New Testament	41
Figure 5: Biblical Reconciliation: Erasing Pre-existing Exclusionary Boundaries and Embracing New Life in the Spirit	43
Table 1: The Experience of Black Pastors: A Journey in Three Stages	69
Table 2: Being Welcomed into the Denomination: Stage One of the Journey	70
Table 3: Experiencing Racial Fatigue as an Outsider: Stage Two of the Journey	75
Table 4: Learning to Thrive: Stage Three of the Journey	102

Foreword

As a young child, I had a clear sense of God's presence. My parents were churchgoers, and as I grew up in the church my desire to please God and follow Jesus increased by leaps and bounds. However, my perceived relationship with God began to fall apart with the growing consciousness that I was a sinner. Instinctively, by the age of six, I knew that to be right with God required living a perfect life, and I already failed to measure up to that standard.

Though the church of my childhood was predominantly African American, it shared most of the characteristics of American Protestantism, including a common vocabulary which sounded abstract to me as a six-year-old. Therefore, the growing rift I perceived between the Lord and myself continued to grow. I cannot count the number of times I was told, "Accept Jesus as your personal savior." However, these words had no point of reference for me as a young child. The use of the King James Bible made matters worse. The meaning of the Bible passages I heard was obscured by its unfamiliar language. If someone had communicated God's plan of salvation in understandable language, I would have gladly received the message.

My church was full of saints who truly loved the Lord, but they did not realize that some of us were unable to jump the cultural and linguistic hurdles that granted access to the word of God and fellowship. This left me with a strong desire for God that was unaddressed by my church. By my teen years, I had developed a disdain for the institutional church and generally drifted away from Christianity to flirt with Islam. Had I completed the journey toward Islam, I would have joined the thousands of young African American men bowing toward Mecca—young men who hungered to be righteous before God, yet saw themselves as former Christians.

Fortunately, I encountered two "out-of-the-church-box" young men who knew Jesus. They not only spoke my language, but were also able to answer the many theological questions that haunted me during my decade-long drift away from the church. Finally, after wrestling with the truth of God's word, I surrendered to Jesus and experienced the joy of God's presence. Only this time, this relationship was based on what Jesus did and said, not just on how I felt. At last, I enjoyed the benefits of Jesus having lived a perfect life for me. These young men who led me to Christ also discipled me, equipping me to communicate and defend the faith in the midst of the surrounding cultural hostility.

I share my faith journey to illustrate a problem with the church in our contemporary context, namely, a failure to communicate. The issue involves more than language. It is compounded by culture, tradition, and ecclesiology. We live in a society that is becoming more diverse by the minute, but in too many cases the American church institution doesn't seem to have gotten the memo. As a result, there is a growing population of people like myself before I met Christ—people who long for God and yet are becoming unchurched and even unchurchable.

We can be thankful for the robust theology that has come to us through the Reformed heritage. However, many times we have been lulled into thinking of theology as merely a noun. Theology is much more than a noun, it is also a verb—something we do in our present context, not merely something we study from history. The same applies to the need for reformation. We can truly be thankful for our sixteenth-century forefathers in the faith who saw the need for a radical reset of the church based on *sola Scriptura*. These theologians freed the Western church from the voluminous junk that had piled up through centuries of tradition and corruption.

It is still true that "all have sinned and fall short of the glory of God" (Rom 3:23). Among other things, this means we have not yet arrived at our God-given destination. The journey continues. "Through many dangers, toils and snares [we] have already come." It was "grace that brought [us] safe thus far and grace will lead [us] home." Until we arrive home, it is not enough to stagnate in our present state of being reformed. The PCA in its present state should continue to seek reformation—seeking better ways of being biblical in our culturally diverse context. After all, we too are subject to the same dynamics of degeneration that led to the need for reformation 500 years ago. The last time I checked, all of us in the body of Christ are still being delivered from our fallen condition.

For some of us, the idea of a continuing reformation is fraught with the dangers, toils, and snares of apostasy. This is a valid observation that must be taken seriously. We have seen examples of apostasy early in the twentieth century, when many mainline denominations were taken over by those who had turned away from the authority of Scripture and subscribed to heresies shaped by humanism and existential make-believe-ism.

Today's flirtation with apostasy is seen among those who blur the distinction between Christian identity and American identity. Many who oppose this do so through Marxist-inspired ideology disguised as theology. Both views are divisive and even apostate because they deny the transcendence of God's kingdom.

We must not forget that failing to see our present need for reform is also fraught with peril. It is easy to slip into the mentality that all the reforming that can be done has been done. Eventually, this can lead to being culture-bound, failing to distinguish between biblical norms derived from the application of God's word and cultural norms arising from tradition. This is also divisive. The negative effects are often felt by brothers and sisters in other cultures who strongly affirm Reformed theology, yet chafe as they learn about some who contradicted this theology by their traditions and practices.

The PCA may claim to adhere to our motto: "faithful to the Scriptures, true to the Reformed Faith, and obedient to the Great Commission," but without biblical wisdom we may end up developing an ossified and disconnected denominational bubble—an ecclesiological establishment out of touch with, and even inhospitable toward, people in other cultural contexts who may be hungering and thirsting after righteousness. The Great Commission remains a matter of making disciples. If we are faithful to this prime directive, the emergence of innovative ways of living out our motto will be the inevitable result and our denomination will serve this movement to the glory of God.

The early church in the book of Acts stands as a reformation paradigm for us today. They exercised covenant faithfulness by caring for widows in need, but cultural differences among these widows revealed a problem with the distribution system. In response, they demonstrated ecclesiological creativity, inaugurating a new church office called "deacon" to sort things out. This was a faithful application of biblical wisdom. "So the word of God spread. The number of disciples in Jerusalem increased rapidly, and a large number of priests became obedient to the faith" (Acts 6:7 NIV). This wise innovation also contributed to the church's ability to break out of the Jewish cultural bubble to become the global body of Christ.

Given the stresses and strains of our current cultural context, it is imperative that we in the PCA seek to continue in the same spirit of the early church—to be biblically sound and ecclesiastically creative. Thank God for Billy Boyce, who has given a thought-provoking contribution to all of us who have serious concerns about the health of the PCA. For all who long to see our denomination realize the lofty aspirations of our motto, *Outsiders on the Inside* is a must read.

CARL F. ELLIS, JR.

Introduction

"Faithful to the Scriptures, True to the Reformed Faith, and Obedient to the Great Commission."
—PCA Motto[1]

"All Races Welcome."
—PCA Formation Steering Committee[2]

At its inception, the Presbyterian Church in American (PCA) faced an important question: What kind of church would the new denomination be? It was the early 1970s, a time of racial and theological tension, and the founders aspired to be a church that would brightly shine the light of the gospel by faithfully upholding the biblical, theological, and missiological heritage of confessional Presbyterianism while welcoming people of all races into worship. These were laudable goals, but time has shown the challenge of turning goals into reality. The tensions present at the PCA's birth continue to impact the denomination. After nearly fifty years of denominational life, has the PCA lived up to their founding commitments?

This is a timely question. In concert with the broader global movement of racial introspection and activism, American churches are wrestling with their histories. Have noble theological commitments coincided with, or even led to, exclusionary church practices? Has such exclusion persisted?

1. Sparkman, "History of PCA Motto," para. 1.
2. Item 47 of the "Minutes of the Advisory Committee," 27.

Leaders are increasingly aware that the story of Christianity is not simply about which theological truths were confessed, but also about who was included in or excluded from the community. In the church, doctrine, mission, and church life are intertwined.[3] For churches that aspire to doctrinal orthodoxy and missiological faithfulness, aspirations must be tempered by analysis, and so reflection is warranted.

This book explores the intertwined story of doctrine, mission, and racial inclusion in the PCA in order to help pastors and congregants understand and assess the church's progress toward racial inclusivity. Though it focuses primarily on one denomination, this analysis offers a method for other church organizations asking similar questions: What does the gospel have to do with race? What does theology have to do with culture? And how can believers of different backgrounds come together in Christian unity?

However, from the outset, many might wonder if we need yet another book written by a White male pastor offering an explanation about race in the church.[4] While I have asked myself this daunting question numerous times throughout this study, my goal is to tread fresh ground by placing the experiences of Black pastors at the center, within the interpretive lenses of both theology and culture. This introduction offers an overview of this method, situating the book within larger conversations of race and church life.

WHY THIS BOOK?

This project began at the intersection of pastoral ministry, theology, and current events. I began researching this material in 2015, just one year after the killings of Michael Brown in Missouri, Eric Garner in New York, and Tamir Rice in Ohio. In the midst of these tumultuous events, I began meeting with

---

3. As chapter 2 will argue, missiological faithfulness necessitates a willingness to pursue racial diversity, in so far as one is able in the context of one's ministry.

4. A note on capitalization: Throughout this project, I have chosen to capitalize both "Black" and "White" when applied to individuals or groups as a descriptor of race. While there are extensive discussions available for making this decision, I have followed the guidance of Dr. Carl Ellis, who made this recommendation in a personal conversation. His rationale is as follows: in earlier times, the word "Negro" would have been used as a descriptor for African Americans and would have been capitalized. As such, Black is to be capitalized to emphasize its use as a proper descriptor of a group of people. Similarly, if one capitalizes Black, one ought to equally capitalize White as a descriptor of a group of people. To capitalize one without the other is to draw more on critical theory than theological anthropology, as all are made in God's image. Using these terms as theologically informed descriptors allows for a uniformity of language, without requiring an ideological hardening, as if capitalizing Black forces one into a racially essentialist paradigm. My thanks to Dr. Ellis for these recommendations.

some local Black pastors, asking the question that became fundamental to this book: "What is it like to be Black in the PCA?" At the same time, I read Herman Bavinck's *The Christian Family*, which offered the theologian's explanation for God's Old Testament prohibitions on incestuous relationships: God designed his creation to move toward greater diversity. Slowly it dawned on me that these conversations were related, since current affairs, church experiences, and theology were asking the same questions: What does God think of the current divisive reality of race relations? Where did these issues come from? Is there a theological analysis that could help bring clarity? As followers of Christ, what role does the church have in promoting healing? I eventually enrolled in a Doctor of Ministry program to ask these questions using a more structured approach, and my dissertation became the first draft of this book.

Entering the national conversation regarding race can be overwhelming. Since beginning this study, numerous high-profile deaths have drawn increased national (and global) attention to the Black Lives Matter movement. With each death, the collective sense of trauma has grown, as has the pressure to make meaningful progress toward justice. The conversation itself, however, is fluid: terminology changes, older terms like "racial reconciliation" are replaced with "racial justice" or "anti-racism," and new research is regularly pumped out, so that one's reading list grows at an overwhelming pace. A quick glance at the bestsellers discussing race reveals a vast array of disciplines and genres: sociology, history, political science, educational theory, theology, memoir, comic book, children's literature, and more. Amid such upheaval, churches and church leaders have struggled to respond.

Church trends mirror such tumultuous social dynamics, while vocabulary develops and relationships shift. As one example of the changing dynamic, during the earliest stages of research, I relied heavily on the Reformed African American Network (RAAN), which emphasized providing a minority voice within multiethnic, Reformed, evangelical churches. However, due to ongoing relational tension within these multiethnic spaces, and a growing disappointment with how White evangelicals tolerated racist comments from national leaders, the network changed direction away from multiethnicity and toward the Black church tradition. This shift was codified in a new name for the organization: from RAAN to "The Witness— A Black Christian Collective." This organizational change coincides with a "quiet exodus" of minority Christians leaving mainstream evangelicalism, citing disenchantment with the majority-White culture's shallow commitment to multiethnicity.[5] This is just one example of the changing intellectual

---

5. Robertson, "Quiet Exodus."

landscape, which also includes an ever-growing list of publications and debated topics.[6]

While these shifting trends and growing resources can lead to a sense of paralysis, it is important for Christians, and especially church leaders, not to give up. Though the landscape is shifting, the fundamentals remain the same, and these fundamentals have their foundation within biblical redemptive history. At critical points in redemptive history, God gives us divine perspective on the questions of our day: from creation to new creation, God enters into our fractured story of race. This conversation, therefore, is central to church life and mission, and church leaders already have the core tools needed to engage.

I believe that the conversation about the church and race is both necessary and possible. As a ministry practitioner, I have sought theologically grounded and practical answers. While this book is conversant with many of the scholarly voices already referenced, I do not attempt to offer either a literature survey or an in-depth, technical analysis of various schools of thought. I am one ministry leader writing to another. Because of this, much of the research presented here takes the form of interviews with other ministry leaders. This is a work of practical theology, exploring the experience of Black pastors who labored through racial fatigue to develop racial resilience. I am convinced that listening is an important part of the analytical process and that their stories help generate a theoretical framework for minority experience.

Listening is also an important part of the pastoral process. This book aims to improve ministry by modeling a constructive conversation about race by attempting to see the world from another's point of view for the sake of reconciliation. As such, it offers a method for overcoming what theologian George Yancey calls "racial gridlock."[7] Based on my observations, this racial gridlock is seen in two conflicting approaches to racially charged situations: the "Stats Response" and the "Story Response."[8] For example, when discussing the phenomenon of "driving while Black," the Stats Response meets experiential evidence with distrust, quickly dismissing the experience by pointing to statistical studies that supposedly debunk the normativity of such an experience. In contrast, the Story Response meets empirical evidence with suspicion, preferring to analyze a specific racially charged

---

6. Notable volumes, all released within the span of one year, include Kwon and Thompson, *Reparations*; McCaulley, *Reading While Black*; Bradley, *Why Black Lives Matter*; and Ince, *Beautiful Community*.

7. Yancey, *Beyond Racial Gridlock*.

8. The following descriptions are overly simplistic but serve to highlight the basic presuppositions of each approach.

incident in the context of larger social narratives. While both responses contain elements of truth, both work against trust. Each approach stems from deeply ingrained and contrasting beliefs, issues judgment on the basis of preconceived ideas, and sees the other as acting with improper racial bias. Neither response can move the conversation beyond racial gridlock; instead, they deepen the divide by perpetuating mistrust.

Listening, in contrast, is a pastorally appropriate way through the gridlock. By processing the experiences of others, Christians from different or divided backgrounds can move away from gridlock and toward *koinonia*—true fellowship and mutual belonging between Christians who understand each other's perspective with empathy and Christian love. Such relationships overcome division with reconciliation, and foster an environment where people of every race can find a welcoming, if still imperfect, place in American churches.

FROM DOCTRINE TO EXPERIENCE

To move toward this ideal of *koinonia* in the church, this book explores two related questions, the first being theological and the second empirical. First, how does doctrine inform racial hospitality? Do the PCA's biblical and theological convictions mandate churches where all races are welcome? This leads to the second question: Do the denomination's minorities experience racial hospitality? For example, do Black PCA pastors experience the denomination to be a place where they, as racial minorities, are welcome? This second question is crucial for true *koinonia*, since it moves the discussion beyond pure theology into the realm of real human relationships.

Answering the first question is the goal of Part I: Racial Hospitality in Scripture and Tradition. Chapter 1 follows the history of the PCA, looking particularly at trends of racial inclusion and exclusion. In the context of church history, the phrase "All Races Welcome" signals an important departure from certain past sins, but also remains a goal yet to be attained. Chapters 2 and 3 move from history to theology, exploring the connections between the PCA's doctrine and its social and theological goals. Chapter 2 studies the trajectory of racial inclusion in biblical theology. Can there be outsiders within the kingdom of God? If not, then biblically all races should be welcomed. Chapter 3 mines the resources of the Reformed tradition, specifically using Herman Bavinck's *Reformed Dogmatics* to investigate connections between racial diversity and God's purposes in the world. Should Reformed churches prize and pursue diversity based on their theological convictions? If so, then, again, all races should be welcomed.

The goals of Part I are straightforward and have immediate application in church contexts. First, exploring race from a theological perspective grounds the ensuing assessment on God's redemptive activity, which preserves several important theological emphases, such as the goodness of creation, the human person as the image of God, the impact of original sin, and the scope of Christ's redemption—all of which are vital concepts for a robust dialogue about race. Second, by showing clear links between doctrine and racial diversity, the pursuit of racial reconciliation becomes an aspect of Christian discipleship and faithfulness. By itself, Part I serves to emphasize a previous point: the conversation about race is both necessary and possible. Church leaders are already equipped with the most important tools for this redemptive pursuit: Scripture and church tradition.

However, these tools must be employed for constructive racial reconciliation: redemptive racial relationships cannot simply be assumed on the basis of an orthodox confession. As will be shown, a commitment to the Bible and to Reformed theology does not automatically translate into a commitment to racial inclusivity.

Part II: Racial Hospitality in the PCA explores the question of the human relationship: Do the PCA's Black pastors experience the welcome that should flow from faithfulness to Scripture and the Reformed tradition? After the resounding "Yes!" to "All Races Welcome" in Part I, Part II offers a more sober portrait of life on the ground. Chapter 4 establishes a methodology for understanding the experience of PCA minority pastors: phenomenology, or the "essence of a lived phenomenon."[9] By allowing the experiences of these Black pastors to frame the discussion, we can more systematically answer the question: "What does it feel like to be Black in the PCA?" In chapters 5–7, several Black pastors share their experiences. From their stories, a picture emerges: to be Black in the PCA is to be caught somewhere between an insider and an outsider. This minority experience exhibits three clear movements: an initial welcome as an insider, a painful realization of still being an outsider, and finally, a decision to learn to thrive. Chapter 8 evaluates these findings in light of the PCA's theological commitments and offers some pastoral conclusions.

This will not be the final word on any and every minority experience. Instead, it models a conversation that must be replicated. You are encouraged to take these questions into your own spheres of influence, asking of others, "What are your racial, ethnic, and cultural experiences?" "What does it feel like to 'be you' in this space?" Such personal questions allow us to corporately engage broader questions: "What is a culture that harms?"

---

9. Creswell and Poth, *Qualitative Inquiry and Research Design*, 104–5.

and "What is a culture that heals?" For evangelical and Reformed churches in particular, this study is a challenge to live purposefully into our biblical, theological, and missiological heritage of welcome and hospitality in order to be a healing presence in a racially fractured world.

Key Terms and Concepts

ETHNICITY AND RACE: *Ethnicity* refers to one's identity as understood through nationality, language, and cultural distinctives, stemming from a relationship to a specific geographical region. *Race* refers to the sociological interpretation of biological, and specifically physical or phenotypic, characteristics. Whereas *ethnic* difference existed in ancient times, *race* is a distinctly modern invention, a concept created to serve modernity's larger preoccupation with mastering creation by discerning certain essential structures.[1] Within modernity, race came to transcend and replace ethnicity as an organizing principle, thereby removing one's relationship to a specific geographical location and grounding one's core identity in skin tone.[2] As a concept, race was invented both to simplify the divisions within humanity and to assert the dominance of the "White race" over others.[3]

RACISM: While it is commonly agreed that race is a sociological interpretation of biological characteristics, defining racism is more challenging. There are numerous definitions, stemming from various schools of thought, but I believe a theological definition deserves primacy. Since the concept of race came from a worldview that sought to define and exploit difference for the sake of one culture's gain, racism is rooted in sin. Therefore the best

---

1. See Carter, *Race*, 79–124.
2. Thus, all Africans became Black, and all Europeans became White. See Jennings, *Christian Imagination*, for reflections on the tragic impact of separating identity from location.
3. Carter shows how the concept of race came pre-loaded with "anti-Black" sentiment (see Carter, *Race*).

definition of it develops from a doctrine of God and humanity. I believe that the definition of race found in the PCA's "Pastoral Letter on Racism" is most accurate:

> Racism is any want of conformity to or transgression of the Bible's approach to race; it is any belief or act that is contrary to God's bringing His redeeming *shalom* to the races. More specifically, racism is the sinful action or attitude of elevating (idolizing) the superiority of one's race over another in such a way as to cause a lack of love for one another as Christ loved, to hate others in our hearts and actions, and/or to act toward a race in an oppressive, unjust or indifferent manner. Racism, like any other sin, is expressed in thoughts and actions by an individual. But as individuals act together, racism can be expressed by a group or institution.[4]

RACIAL RECONCILIATION: Since race and racism are ultimately theological distortions, the solution to racism must be theological in nature. Racial reconciliation begins with God's desire to unite all nations as one people, a desire that takes flesh in the person and ministry of Christ, and becomes a living reality through the power of the Spirit. Building trust between individuals of different races and ethnicities, along with replacing sinful division with fellowship and love, are theological and redemptive works. At an individual level this occurs through redemptive relationships, while at the institutional level this occurs as cultures of systemic, habitual exclusion are transformed to become ones of systemic, habitual inclusion.[5]

---

4. Committee on Mission to North America, "Pastoral Letter on Racism," 8.

5. Even though the term "racial reconciliation" is considered by some to be outdated or incorrect, it remains helpful in this project for two reasons. First, it is appropriate biblical-theological language for the restoration of relationships (e.g., Eph 2:14–17), and second, it is the preferred language of the PCA's documents (e.g., the Racial and Ethnic Reconciliation Study Committee). For a critique of racial reconciliation, see Charles, "10 Reasons Why I'm Switching." For a defense of the term, see Kwon, "Should We Abandon the Language of 'Racial Reconciliation?'"

PART I

Racial Hospitality in Scripture and Tradition

1

All Races Welcome?

WHAT IS IT LIKE to be Black in the PCA? After asking this question multiple times, the most common answer was, "It's complicated." For Black pastors, their ministry is marked by tension. As an ultra-minority in the denomination, they experience what W. E. B. du Bois calls "double consciousness."[1] They are fully aware of their identity as Black Presbyterians—Presbyterians, yes, but specifically *Black* Presbyterians. They have a right to be in this denomination—after all, Black Presbyterianism has existed in the United States since at least the year 1800.[2] And yet, these seminary-trained, biblically grounded, and theologically Reformed men often feel alienated within the denomination.[3]

Statistically speaking, this might be expected. When one is an ultra-minority, a member of only 1 percent of the denomination's pastors, it is likely—however lamentable—that a sense of alienation will be experienced.[4] But statistics only tell part of the story. It is not simply a question of smaller numbers, but of cultural divides. Recent developments in the denomination

---

1. du Bois, *Souls of Black Folk*, 2. The phrase "ultra-minority" came from an interview with "Brian"; see chapter 4 for more information about the interviews.

2. PCA Mission to North America, "History of African American Presbyterianism."

3. See Bradley, *Aliens in the Promised Land*.

4. As of the time of writing, there were 57 Black pastors out of roughly 5,100 total pastors. The total number of ministers was obtained from the PCA's Five-Year Summary. The number of Black pastors was obtained directly from the African American Ministries coordinator.

have brought this division to light. For example, the PCA recently commissioned a study report on race and reconciliation in the denomination, but this report revealed that the denomination was divided on the very need to study the issue at all. According to the report, "Those ages 50+, those living in Southern states and those with less education rated the need [for a study on race] significantly lower than other groups. Caucasians, Latino/Hispanic and Other ethnicities rated the need significantly lower than African Americans and Asian-Americans."[5] In other words, the denomination's leadership cannot agree on the need to have a conversation about race at all, let alone how to have it well. As a result, African American Teaching Elders in the PCA feel disconnected from the majority because of culture, not simply numbers. For a denomination that declared the church would "welcome fellow believers in Christ regardless of race," this is lamentable.[6] Given the historical roots of the denomination, however, it might not be unexpected. The story of the PCA has never been strictly doctrinal. For Presbyterians in the United States, culture often intersected with doctrine to oppose full racial inclusion.

CIVIL WAR AND SOUTHERN PRESBYTERIAN RACISM

To understand the PCA, we need to understand the PCA's Southern heritage. The PCA traces its roots back to the Southern Presbyterian Church, which had a history of racial exclusion. Just months after the beginning of the American Civil War in 1861, the Presbyterian Church in the United States of America, which included churches in both North and South, adopted the Gardiner-Spring Resolution. This resolution required all churches in the denomination to support the United States federal government—the Union—or face church censure. For churches in secessionist southern states, this created an inescapable dilemma: support what was, in their minds, a foreign power, or face discipline.[7] These southern churches decided to sever

---

5. Presbyterian Church in America, "Report of the Ad Interim Committee," 2445. To complicate this divide further, it is not simply cultural background that indicates one's perceived need for a study, but also church role. Within the PCA, there are two classes of leadership: Teaching Elders (TEs), who are ordained clergy, and Ruling Elders (REs), who are lay leaders. According to this study, TEs were twice as likely as REs to identify a need to study race and reconciliation: 31 percent of TE respondents thought that the establishment of the study committee was "extremely needed." Conversely, only 15 percent of RE respondents felt that this was "extremely needed."

6. Item 47 of the "Minutes of the Advisory Committee," 27.

7. Lucas, *On Being Presbyterian*, 196.

ecclesial ties and form a new denomination rooted in the Confederacy: the Presbyterian Church in the Confederate States of America (CSA).[8]

These leaders attempted to rationalize their decision with an appeal to doctrine. For them, the Gardiner-Spring Resolution overstepped a fundamental doctrine: the "spirituality of the church." This doctrine stated that the church as institution could only speak to spiritual matters, not political ones.[9] To these leaders, an ecclesial decree requiring churches to take sides politically, pledging allegiance to a specific governing authority during a time of national fracturing, clearly transgressed the denomination's limited authority. So, with their "Address to All the Churches of Jesus Christ Throughout the Earth," the Confederates birthed their new church, founded upon the doctrine of the spirituality of the church.[10] Yet, even within this document, it became clear that while the Confederates utilized doctrine to resist the encroachment of one culture, they equally utilized doctrine to protect the practices of their own culture.

The newly founded denomination wasted no time declaring its stance on slavery. Having declared their grievances with the Northern Church on the first three pages of "Address to All the Churches," the Southern Presbyterians spend the next four pages detailing their justification for slavery. First, God's word does not explicitly condemn slavery, and so the church ought not as well: "[The church] has planted itself upon the word of God, and utterly refused to make slaveholding a sin, or non-slave holding a term of communion."[11] Because, in their view, God's word did not explicitly condemn slavery, it was a civil matter, not an ecclesial one; and as a civil matter, the church had no standing to comment on the institution: "The policy of its existence or non-existence is a question which exclusively belongs to the State. We have no right, as a Church, to enjoin it as a duty, or to condemn it as a sin."[12]

What the Confederate church could comment on, however, was the relationship between slaves and slave owners: "Our business is with the duties which spring from the relation; the duties of the masters on the one hand, and of their slaves on the other. These duties we are to proclaim and

---

8. Taylor, "Spirituality of the Church," 6.

9. Lucas, *On Being Presbyterian*, 196. See also Lucas, *For a Continuing Church*, 39.

10. This address, which functionally declared the separation and founding of the Confederate Church, spends three full pages delineating the distinction between the state and the church as rationale for the Southern accusation that the Northern Church overstepped the spirituality of the church (Wilson, *Presbyterian Historical Almanac*, 427–30).

11. Wilson, *Presbyterian Historical Almanac*, 431.

12. Wilson, *Presbyterian Historical Almanac*, 431–32.

enforce with spiritual sanctions."[13] Condemning slavery as a sin ostensibly created a pastoral problem, as the Southerners would not be able to minister to the slaves in their midst: "We feel that the souls of our slaves are a solemn trust, and we shall strive to present them faultless and complete before the presence of God."[14] But this pastoral obligation was embedded in the racism of the South. These Southerners felt that slavery was God's kindness to an inferior and pagan race. Through their enslavement, God allowed these Africans to have contact with Christianity and civilization:

> The general operation of the system [of slavery] is kindly and benevolent; it is a real and effective discipline, and without it, we are profoundly persuaded that the African race in the midst of us can never be elevated in the scale of being. As long as that race, in its comparative degradation, co-exists, side by side, with the White, bondage is its normal condition.[15]

This final statement shows how cultural racism impacted their application of doctrine. Up to this point, one could argue that the Southern cause was legitimate. The American Presbyterians did hold to a separation of church and state, and on the surface, the biblical narrative is frequently unclear on its stance concerning slavery.[16] The Old Testament community was allowed to have slaves, and the New Testament does not directly overturn the practice, so there could be theoretical grounds to place slavery within the realm of civil, rather than ecclesial authority. However, at this point in the document, the Confederate Presbyterians explicitly show that their resistance to the Gardiner-Spring Resolution and their commitment to slavery flow directly from a culture of racism. Indeed, many of the most influential Southern theologians demonstrate explicit racism in their personal work. Robert Lewis Dabney, possibly the most prominent Southern Presbyterian theologian, "was a staunch defender of slavery, demonstrating an intense racial pride that led to fears of 'blood-mixing.'"[17] Thus, the Confederate Presbyterians willingly used doctrine to protect their cultural, and sinful, concerns.

After the Civil War, the Confederate church was renamed the Presbyterian Church in the United States (PCUS), simply known as the Southern

---

13. Wilson, *Presbyterian Historical Almanac*, 431–32.

14. Wilson, *Presbyterian Historical Almanac*, 433.

15. Wilson, *Presbyterian Historical Almanac*, 434.

16. For a simple example regarding the separation of church and state in American Presbyterianism, see the revisions to the Westminster Confession in the 1729 Adopting Act (PCA Historical Center, "The Adopting Act of 1729," § 9).

17. Lucas, *Robert Lewis Dabney*, 17.

Church. But this was far from a fresh start. While the war ended the question of slavery, the church failed to end the question of racial equality:[18] "as many Whites sought to restore the racial hierarchy after the Thirteenth Amendment ended the peculiar institution, segregation became the slavery substitute."[19] Just as they had used doctrine to protect the racist institution of slavery, the Southern Presbyterians now used doctrine to protect the racist institution of Jim Crow.[20] They crafted a "theological case for segregation [with] four overlapping legs: the curse of Noah, divine approval for geographical segregation and disapproval of miscegenation, the biblically mandated cultural segregation, and Jesus's implicit support for segregation."[21] With a supposedly biblical justification for segregation, Southern Presbyterians again invoked the doctrine of the spirituality of the church, labeling these racist practices as civil concerns, not spiritual.[22] According to them, "the Gospel of Jesus Christ concerned sin and salvation, not ethics, morality, and social policies."[23]

CIVIL RIGHTS AND THE FORMATION OF THE PCA

With this individualized, privatized version of the gospel, and the commitment to a spiritual nature of the church, many Southern Christians continued to support racial segregation throughout the Civil Rights era.[24] During this era, rifts that had been latent since the late 1890s resurfaced within the PCUS, as the denomination moved increasingly toward progressive

---

18. This is in keeping with the parallel trajectory of the larger United States. As Isabel Wilkerson points out in remarkable detail, racism was alive and well everywhere, even though it was most explicit in the South (See Wilkerson, *Warmth of Other Suns*).

19. Taylor, "Spirituality of the Church," 6.

20. This may be an unnecessarily cynical view of the doctrine of "the spirituality of the church"; some scholars have attempted to show that the link between racism and doctrine was more complicated. For more on this, see Lucas, *Robert Lewis Dabney*, 93–94. Other scholars take a more pessimistic view of the matter, stating that the doctrine was merely a fabrication to cover their overt racism. For this take, see Slade, *Open Friendship in a Closed Society*, 94.

21. Taylor, "Spirituality of the Church," 8.

22. Taylor, "Spirituality of the Church," 12.

23. Taylor, "Spirituality of the Church," 13. See also Lucas, *For a Continuing Church*, 40.

24. This claim ultimately leads some scholars to believe that evangelical theology itself lacks the resources to adequately address the racial tensions present in our day. Theirs is a theological claim that warrants further study (See Dupont, "Jim Crow, Civil Rights").

theological and social stances.[25] A church that had largely been a bastion of conservative theology began debating issues that had historically been settled, including biblical inerrancy, the centralization of church government, the ordination of female clergy, and the question of racial integration in the church.[26] As the denomination moved further toward adopting progressive stances on these issues, a frustrated minority of conservatives emerged who clung to the spirit of the older Southern theological traditions on these doctrinal and social issues.[27]

As before, these leaders utilized theology to protect a cultural commitment. On the question of race, they were openly opposed to the activism of the Civil Rights movement, citing the spirituality of the church as the theological rationale to uphold segregation in both society and church.[28] This ecclesiology "helped adherents frame their opposition to civil rights efforts as high-minded theological commitments to the church's true mission."[29] Simultaneously, their privatized view of the gospel allowed them to proclaim that "the heart of the gospel is not the treatment of others, but. . . . 'Believe on the Lord Jesus Christ.'"[30] These Southern Presbyterian conservatives particularly resented clergy who became involved in the Civil Rights movement. They opposed Northern clergy who marched in protests, drawing on the old Southern doctrines to state that there was "no biblical warrant for ministers marching in picket lines"; in their minds, many clergy seemed "more interested in righting social and political wrongs, real or imagined, than in preaching the gospel and saving sinners."[31] They opposed integration in broader society and were particularly fearful of interracial marriage.[32] When the Supreme Court demanded school integration in 1964, Southern churches started their own private schools, often under the label of resisting government overreach, but these schools remained segregated.[33] They also opposed racial integration of church congregations, with one congregation

25. Lucas, *For a Continuing Church*, 12–38.
26. See Lucas, *For a Continuing Church*, 84–89, 103, 207–12, and 112–26.
27. See, e.g., chapter 4 of Lucas, *For a Continuing Church*, entitled "'How Far Will the Progressives Go?' The Coalescing of Conservative Dissent," 66–100.
28. Lucas, *For a Continuing Church*, 112–26 and 182–88.
29. Dupont, *Mississippi Praying*, 188.
30. Dupont, *Mississippi Praying*, 215. This exposition comes from two Southern Presbyterian pastors, B. I. Anderson and Dr. John Reed Miller, writing in 1964.
31. Presbyterian elder Leonard Lowrey, quoted in Dupont, *Mississippi Praying*, 190. Note here the presence of the doctrine of the spirituality of the church in his divorce of social wrongs and the preaching of the gospel.
32. Lucas, *For a Continuing Church*, 116–20.
33. Dupont, *Mississippi Praying*, 217–18; Lucas, *For a Continuing Church*, 213.

expressing its desire "to continue the policy of not allowing all races, creeds, and colors entrance to the worship services of this church."[34] Some churches went so far as to post deacons and elders at the church doors to prevent integration of services.[35] With these extreme measures in service of an openly racist position, these Southern Presbyterians further demonstrated the intermingling of doctrine and culture.

Despite the protestations of conservative Southern leaders, the PCUS slowly slid toward liberalism. These conservatives blamed liberal theology for the increasingly progressive social agenda of the church, so they banded together to create a new denomination committed to Scripture, the Great Commission, and the original Presbyterian movement.[36] In 1972, there was a mass withdrawal from the PCUS, forming what is now known as the Presbyterian Church in America (PCA). In its own inaugural announcement, "A Message to All Churches of Jesus Christ Throughout the World," the new denomination cited "a diluted theology, a gospel tending toward humanism, an unbiblical view of marriage and divorce, the ordination of women, financing of abortion on socio-economic grounds, and numerous other non-Biblical positions ... all traceable to a different view of Scripture from that we hold and that which was held by the Southern Presbyterian forefathers" as their rationale for separating and forming this new denomination.[37]

Notably absent from this declaration is any explicit reference to race relations, even though, as noted at the beginning, the new denomination's steering committee explicitly called for racial inclusion. However, even that desire seems at best inconsistent with the actions and words of some of the PCA's founders, who expressed open antipathy toward the goals of the Civil Rights movement.[38] Their arguments show a form of development. Unlike their Confederate forefathers, who argued for segregation in explicitly racist terms, the newer arguments attempted to center on Scripture rather than

---

34. Session of Alta Woods Presbyterian Church, quoted in Dupont, *Mississippi Praying*, 215.

35. Haynes, *Last Segregated Hour*, 56, 109–12. Haynes's work demonstrates the conflict generated by the Session's decision to block church integration, as many in the church disagreed with the leadership's policy.

36. Lucas, *For a Continuing Church*, 281–83.

37. National Presbyterian Church, "Message to All Churches of Jesus Christ." Note: The National Presbyterian Church soon changed its name to the Presbyterian Church in America. It is also worth noting their symbolic channeling of the Southern Presbyterian Church, as the inaugural address of the Presbyterian Church (CSA) was entitled "Address to All the Churches of Jesus Christ Throughout the Earth." Whether this intentional nod to the Old School Southern Presbyterians included their views on race is up for debate.

38. Dupont, *Mississippi Praying*, 217–18.

prejudice. They cited biblical sources for the separation of races and touted perceived social benefits for both races, instead of citing the superiority or inferiority of either race.[39] This allowed them to dodge the charge of racism while still supporting social positions that implicitly allowed racism to flourish.

This development mirrored the shifting landscape within US race relations. The culture moved from the explicit, overt racism of slavery and Jim Crow, toward the implicit or "institutionalized" racism of post-Jim Crow America.[40] While this is overall a positive development, it should not be understood as racial healing. Indeed, many of the previous cultural divides have remained, and it is much harder to diagnose implicit racism within a church, or to establish that a leader's beliefs were indeed racist. The old tension between theology and culture persists, creating an environment of anxiety surrounding ethical issues, like race.

1982: A JOINING OF NORTH AND SOUTH

Despite this ongoing tension, the PCA has made great strides toward racial reconciliation. It was no small matter for a denomination with roots in the Confederacy to declare that all races were welcome in worship. In 1982, the PCA further enriched this commitment by merging with a sister denomination, the Reformed Presbyterian Church, Evangelical Synod (RPCES), whose heritage was primarily Northern. This joining and receiving was significant on multiple levels, but of relevance here is the RPCES's track record on race relations. In 1966, while some Southern Presbyterians were physically blocking church entrances to prevent worship integration, the RPCES adopted the "Report on Racial Questions." This report specifically named intentional segregation in worship a sin, labeling acceptance of other believers as evidence of God's love and a believer's genuine salvation.[41] The study also debunked scriptural defenses of segregation and even supported interracial marriage, while also acknowledging the difficulties that might stem from such unions.[42] This is in contrast to many Southern Presbyterians, who argued for segregation in society, worship, and family to preserve

---

39. Dupont, *Mississippi Praying*, 217–18. See also Lucas, *For a Continuing Church*, 116–18.

40. Sechrest, "Racism," 655. Sechrest defines institutionalized racism as "the way that material, attitudes, emotions, habits, and practices are imbedded [with]in social institutions."

41. RPCES, "Report on Racial Questions."

42. RPCES, "Report on Racial Questions."

peace.⁴³ The RPCES, in stark contrast to the conservative Presbyterianism stemming from the Civil War South, saw racial issues as moral issues requiring church involvement.

The RPCES also provided multiethnic churches to the PCA. Notable RPCES congregations were actively committed to racial reconciliation, such as New City Fellowship in Chattanooga, Tennessee. The founders of this congregation "wrestled with the oddities of living in the still strange, unofficially segregated South and its biblical calling to pursue reconciliation and ministry among the urban poor" and were "determined to do something about it."⁴⁴ The RPCES also produced for the PCA leaders committed to the cause of racial reconciliation, including Dr. Carl Ellis, Jr., who longed to see an "indigenous Reformed movement in the African American community" that applied Reformed theology to cultural concerns.⁴⁵ Thus, the joining and receiving increased the PCA's momentum toward achieving its aim of racially integrated churches.

DECLARATIONS OF PROGRESS

Other landmark events in the history of the PCA took place in 2002 and 2004. In 2002, the General Assembly (GA) adopted a statement of confession and repentance concerning the sin of slavery.⁴⁶ This "Racial Reconciliation Position Paper" declares that "the heinous sins attendant with unbiblical forms of servitude—including oppression, racism, exploitation, manstealing, and chattel slavery—stand in opposition to the Gospel" and that "the effects of these sins have created and continue to create barriers between brothers and sisters of different races and/or economic spheres and the aftereffects of these sins continue to be felt in the economic, cultural,

---

43. Arguments in favor of segregation in the name of peace can be found in Taylor, "Spirituality of the Church," 15.

44. Green, "New City Fellowship Chattanooga, Tennessee," para. 3.

45. Tisby, "Indigenous Reformed Movement," para 1. For testimony concerning Dr. Ellis's influence within this indigenous movement, see Tisby, "Know Your Black Presbyterians, Pt. 1."

46. General Assembly is the PCA's annual meeting of church elders, a gathering of worship and business. Decisions at the GA level carry significant weight for the denomination, though as a grassroots denomination, culture change is rarely top-down. With no centralized government to issue statements on behalf of the denomination, new denominational statements are received by vote. Though these denominational statements shape precedent, they are not always binding for individual churches.

and social affairs of the communities in which we live and minister."[47] The paper concludes with a dramatic call to repentance and renewal:

> We therefore confess our involvement in these sins. As a people, both we and our fathers, have failed to keep the commandments, the statutes, and the laws God has commanded. We therefore publicly repent of our pride, our complacency, and our complicity. Furthermore, we seek the forgiveness of our brothers and sisters for the reticence of our hearts that have constrained us from acting swiftly in this matter. We will strive, in a manner consistent with the Gospel imperatives, for the encouragement of racial reconciliation, the establishment of urban and minority congregations, and the enhancement of existing ministries of mercy in our cities, among the poor, and across all social, racial, and economic boundaries, to the glory of God. Amen.[48]

In 2004, the GA adopted the "Pastoral Letter on Racism" to "clarify the position of our denomination on very important issues relating to racism in the past, present, and future."[49] The letter goes further than the 2002 position paper by offering a deeper engagement with definitions and theological categories. Most striking is its broad and deep definition of racism:

> Racism is any want of conformity to or transgression of the Bible's approach to race; it is any belief or act that is contrary to God's bringing His redeeming *shalom* to the races. More specifically, racism is the sinful action or attitude of elevating (idolizing) the superiority of one's race over another in such a way as to cause a lack of love for one another as Christ loved, to hate others in our hearts and actions, and/or to act toward a race in an oppressive, unjust or indifferent manner. Racism, like any other sin, is expressed in thoughts and actions by an individual. But as individuals act together, racism can be expressed by a group or institution.[50]

Considering their history up to this point, this definition is stunning. First, by taking up the theological language of the *Westminster Shorter Catechism*, the pastoral letter brings a uniquely Presbyterian theological angle to the problem of racism, placing this document firmly in the stream of Presbyterian thought, while simultaneously correcting a large piece of

---

47. PCA, "Racial Reconciliation," 262.
48. PCA, "Racial Reconciliation," 262
49. Committee on Mission to North America, "Pastoral Letter on Racism," 1.
50. Committee on Mission to North America, "Pastoral Letter on Racism," 8.

American Presbyterian tradition that viewed race merely as a social issue.[51] Second, by invoking the ideal of *shalom*, the document takes the sin of racism further than merely external signs of hatred.[52] Finally, this definition addresses the reality that organizations can be guilty of sin. This final piece would become an important part of later discussions, as the PCA began to explore the question of sin and repentance at the institutional level.

Both the 2002 and 2004 documents were adopted by the denomination, giving these views institutional credibility. However, the votes did not come without controversy. The *Presbyterian and Reformed News*, an independent journal focused primarily on covering the PCA, published several articles covering the 2002 GA debates. One article covers the actual debate at the Assembly, demonstrating the nature of opposition to the position paper. Dissenting voices cited various reasons for voting against the resolution: the need to only repent of personal sins, a fear of undermining the gospel ministry of godly men from the past, blaming the interventions of the federal government for inciting the majority of racial animosity, and a sense that the denomination had been "tainted by unwholesome contemporary influences."[53] This edition of *P&R News* also published an interview with Dr. Morton Smith, one of the founders of the denomination and an avowed Southerner. In this interview, he opined that statements like the position paper struck at the church's Southern heritage by undermining the "spirituality of the church."[54]

However, those who argued against racial reconciliation citing the spirituality of the church did not always apply this doctrine consistently. At the same 2002 GA, the PCA voted against a resolution that would condemn the League of the South, a paleo-Confederate organization wanting

---

51. *Westminster Shorter Catechism*, 14. "Q: What is sin? A: Sin is any want of conformity unto, or transgression of, the law of God."

52. This is also in line with the Reformed tradition, seen in the *Westminster Larger Catechism*, of meditating on the deeper meaning of God's commandments and avoiding a mere external reading of transgressions of God's Law. This tradition roots its method in Jesus's exposition of the Ten Commandments, especially in Matthew 5:21–48.

53. P&R News, "Assembly Adopts Racial Reconciliation Overture," 4. Interestingly, the elder who made this final comment would eventually be brought up on charges of racism and would leave the denomination, but the fight to bring him to ecclesial trial was itself an ordeal that evidenced the intertwined nature of culture and theology. Even in the midst of the trial, hints of the "spirituality of the church" came up; though this elder's writings undoubtedly communicated a disdain for those of African descent, a fellow church member opined: "I just felt like [his] opinions was [sic] not something addressed specifically in the Scriptures and therefore he had a right to hold them." This is simply more evidence of the difficulty in addressing racial issues from the Southern Presbyterian tradition. See Banks, "Church Confronts, Expels Member," para. 19.

54. P&R News, "Interview with Morton Smith," 14–15.

to resurrect vestiges of the Old South. One of the grounds given for voting against this resolution was the spirituality of the church, namely, that the church ought not comment on a political organization. Yet, one day later, the same Assembly voted to sustain a report calling it a sin for women to serve in combat roles in the military, undeniably a civil affair.[55] The old tension between theology and culture continued to hamper the denomination's efforts to adequately position racial reconciliation within Christian ethics.

The most recent chapter in the journey of racial reconciliation began at the 2015 GA. Two prominent elders presented a "Personal Resolution on Civil Rights Remembrance," taking aim at some of the deficiencies in the 2002 and 2004 documents. Because those previous documents had a tight focus on slavery, they neglected to address "the covenantal, generational, heinous sins committed during the much more recent Civil Rights era," stating that many "conservative Presbyterian churches at the time not only failed to support the Civil Rights movement, but actively worked against racial reconciliation in both church and society."[56]

With this indictment, the resolution then called for three points of action. First, a denominational confession to "recognize and confess our church's covenantal and generational involvement in and complicity with racial injustice inside and outside of our churches during the Civil Rights period."[57] Second, a recommitment "to the task of truth and reconciliation with our African American brothers and sisters for the glory of God and the furtherance of the Gospel."[58] Third, a local manifestation of this institutional repentance, as "congregations of the Presbyterian Church in America . . . confess their own particular sins and failures as may be appropriate and . . . seek to further truth and reconciliation for the gospel's sake within their own local communities."[59]

After much debate, this document was tabled for one year, allowing time for presbyteries to perfect the language and clarify the authors' intentions. Significantly, when compared with the 2002 debates, the reason for

---

55. See P&R News, "Assembly Refuses to Receive Personal Resolution in Opposition to League of the South," 5, and P&R News, "Assembly Goes on Record as Being Opposed to Women in Combat," 6.

56. Lucas and Duncan, "Personal Resolution," para. 2.

57. Lucas and Duncan, "Personal Resolution," para. 7.

58. Lucas and Duncan, "Personal Resolution," para. 8.

59. Lucas and Duncan, "Personal Resolution," para. 9. This is a particularly bold comment, as numerous churches in the PCA followed the trend of "White flight," moving from the city to the suburbs. One notable attempt to fight against this trend was from Francis Schaeffer, who threatened to resign from Covenant Presbyterian Church in St. Louis if they relocated to the suburbs (See Duriez, *Francis Schaeffer*, 40).

tabling was not due to rampant dissention, but largely out of a desire to make progress by gaining clarity and consensus. In a particularly moving speech, TE Jim Baird, one of the original elders of the denomination, confessed the sins of the founders in neglecting this crucial aspect of ministry:

> In 1971 twelve men were elected to form a new denomination. Take two years and form that denomination. Of those twelve men, six were ministers and six were ruling elders. All have died or left the PCA except two: Kennedy Smartt and me. And I confess, that in 1973, the only thing I understood was that we were starting a new denomination, which we did. And I confess that I did not raise a finger for Civil Rights. I was taught . . . one thing, and that was to start a new denomination, for the sake of the Scripture, for the sake of the preservation of historic Presbyterianism, and for the furtherance of the gospel proclamation. And so I confess my sin. I'm not confessing the sin of my fathers, I'm confessing my sin, and of those twelve men. Were we racists? No. But we did not do anything to help our Black brethren.[60]

This personal resolution fueled a burst of activity in the denomination on the subject of race. In 2016, the modified letter was approved by the GA. In 2017, the first Asian American was elected moderator at the annual GA. In 2018, the GA elected the first African American moderator and approved the first full-length study on race in the denomination's history: the Racial and Ethnic Reconciliation Study Committee Report.[61]

At the same time, there continues to be much debate about the PCA's history and the relationship between culture and doctrine. Many objections from the past were leveled at the 2015 Personal Resolution: people need to repent only for their own sins, racism is specifically hatred of others, and the document strikes at the spirituality of the church.[62] The debate had come

---

60. LeCroy, "Transcript of Rev. Jim Baird's Speech," paras. 1–3

61. PCA, "Racial and Ethnic Reconciliation."

62. LeCroy, "The [GA] Protest of 2015." See especially paragraph 3 for a description of the dissenting viewpoints. I have also been in several online discussions about this topic, and these main points come up frequently. These are, of course, the more charitable critiques. The view that the 2015 Personal Resolution has more to do with political correctness than theological correctness is expressed in the satirical piece, "PCA Repents for Failure to Demand Onesimus' Freedom." This particular critique comes from the perspective of the White supremacist movement known as Kinism (See Henry, "PCA Repents"). Interestingly, this Kinist publication at another location cites Morton Smith favorably by republishing his essay "The Racial Problem Facing America," with the following commentary: "Dr. Smith is a highly regarded Reformed Christian theologian, and it should be noted that his words from 1964 do not necessarily reflect his current views, nor should the republication of this article by Tribal

full circle, confirming Faulkner's wisdom that "the past is never dead. It's not even past."[63]

A NEW BATTLE LINE: CRITICAL THEORY IN THE CHURCH

In more recent years, new definitions have further complicated the debate. Previously, the church debated the Bible's place in the discussion. Newer debates concern the value of other analytical tools. At both scholarly and popular levels, the conversation on race has become punctuated by debate about the use of analytical concepts such as privilege, power, intersectionality, and Critical Race Theory (CRT). In other words, the PCA now has two questions to answer: "Should we talk about race?" and "*How* should we talk about race?"

Two public statements clearly illustrate this problem. Following the violence surrounding the "Unite the Right" rally in Charlottesville, Virginia in 2017, two contrasting statements on race appeared from evangelical Reformed groups.[64] Each invited individuals and church leaders to become signatories, and each received many signatures from leaders in the PCA. The Reformed African American Network—now The Witness BCC[65]—published "The Charlottesville Declaration" (hereafter, simply "the Declaration"[66]) on August 25, 2017.[67] The Declaration, authored by two

---

Theocrat be interpreted as any sort of endorsement of this site by Dr. Smith. While I generally find this essay to be an excellent exposition of Kinist principles, it errs in a few points" (Smith, "Racial Problem Facing America," para. 1). This explicit connection with Dr. Smith and Kinism is yet another example of skeletons in the PCA's closet, subtly suggesting to minorities that they are outsiders in the denomination.

63. Faulkner, *Requiem for a Nun*, 73.

64. For more on the events in Charlottesville surrounding this controversial rally, see Katz, "Unrest in Virginia."

65. See the introduction for the context of this change.

66. This is not to be confused with the "Theological Declaration on Christian Faith and White Supremacy" (or simply "#TheDeclaration"), which comes out of the more Anabaptist-leaning circles of *Sojourners*, the New Monasticism, and the "Red Letter Christian" movement. An analysis of this text is outside the scope of this book, but would offer a fascinating countertext to the two statements considered here. Drawing on the Anabaptist tradition, the primary evaluative lens in this text is that of "kingdom," so that White supremacy is a form of cultural imperialism and redemption comes in the form of liberation from such ideological colonialism. Thus, #TheDeclaration is, among other things, a helpful example of hermeneutics in action from outside of the Reformed tradition. A cursory reading of the signatories shows there is little overlap between "the Declaration" and #TheDeclaration. Unfortunately, our religious divisions continue to challenge our ability to overcome racial division.

67. Rhodes and Tisby, "Black Ministers Release Charlottesville Declaration."

African American scholars, names its target directly: "White supremacy." According to the Declaration, Charlottesville was just another manifestation of this national sin, which has been present "from the founding of [America]."[68] The term "White supremacy" appears almost once per paragraph. Similar terms are used at least once, including "racial inequality," "racism," and "White privilege." Far from being merely a sociological term, however, White supremacy is named as a spiritual ailment. The Declaration diagnoses the spiritual underpinnings of White supremacy using biblical terms: it is "the idolatry of Whiteness," a "[suppression of] the truth of God," "out of step with the true Gospel," an expression of "the kingdom of darkness" and "the spirit of the age" that is deserving of "God's justice and judgment."[69]

For the Declaration, White supremacy is antithetical to the gospel. The real gospel will be a sufficient cure, only if it is the "full-orbed Gospel of evangelism and activism."[70] Recovery of this "full-orbed Gospel" for the sake of the nation would entail three acts. First, White pastors must condemn the sin of White supremacy: "nothing less than a full-throated condemnation can lead to true reconciliation in the Lord's body."[71] Second, communities of color must prophetically preach "the personal and social power of the Gospel."[72] Third, both Whites and people of color must make use of the history of the American church to discover "the ways in which

---

68. Rhodes and Tisby, "Black Ministers Release Charlottesville Declaration," para. 1.

69. Rhodes and Tisby, "Black Ministers Release Charlottesville Declaration," paras. 1, 2, 2, 5, 3, 2.

70. Rhodes and Tisby, "Black Ministers Release Charlottesville Declaration," para. 5.

71. Rhodes and Tisby, "Black Ministers Release Charlottesville Declaration," para. 6. This statement hints that the Declaration is not simply trying to address violence between non-Christians; it is not simply that racial strife is taking place "out there," but first of all "in here." While the Declaration does have its main focus on national violence, it subtly suggests that the sinful division on display in Charlottesville is simultaneously mirrored in the life of the body. At the same time, the rhetorical shift from talking about the national problem to the ecclesial problem could be twisted to imply a subtle universalism ("all people are God's children") that is common in progressive Christian circles (i.e., #TheDeclaration and some of its signatories). While a gracious reader will not attribute such universalism to Tisby and Rhodes's work (after all, this was written within the context of evangelicalism), at play in this discussion is language itself. As we will see, the more traditional/conservative approach strongly resists all language of race as used in the broader culture. Therefore, by deploying such terms here, the Declaration loses the capacity to build bridges with the more conservative approach, and unfortunately becomes the target of conservative Christian ire.

72. Rhodes and Tisby, "Black Ministers Release Charlottesville Declaration," para. 7.

the church both legitimized and resisted White supremacy throughout the last several centuries."[73]

On August 31, six days after the Declaration was released, another public statement was issued, but from a very different viewpoint and with a different cohort of signatories. Co-authored by a White Reformed scholar and an African American PCA pastor, "Critical Theory and the Unity of the Church"[74] (hereafter "CT Statement") seeks to correct what the authors see as an imbalance in the approach utilized by the Declaration. While not pointing to the Declaration by name, the CT Statement authors believe that any discussion of race falls short when it relies on analytical tools outside of biblical theology and church tradition.

According to these authors, the critical theory built upon "the power-analysis tradition . . . [of] Marx, Foucault, and others," and which underlies terms such as "'White privilege,' 'White guilt,' [and] 'intersectionality,'" ultimately leads to "divisive identity politics" instead of true reconciliation.[75] According to the CT Statement, critical theory cannot bring reconciliation, in part because it lacks nuance. For example, the CT Statement notes that the idea of White privilege does not do justice to the privileges that other people of color possess. Furthermore, it "reduc[es] the complexity of social relationships to issues of power," dividing "human society into oppressors and oppressed."[76] Finally, with a myopic focus on Whiteness, a racial double-standard is established, in which "only White people can be racists."[77] According to the CT Statement, this secular approach, adopted uncritically by well-meaning but misguided Christians—even within the "conservative Reformed community"—cannot bring people together, but only further divides.

After attempting to show the deficiencies of critical theory, the CT Statement offers an alternative tool for reconciliation: the Christian biblical-theological tradition, specifically the doctrines of creation, sin, incarnation, and church reconciliation. The doctrine of creation teaches that value and identity come from being made in God's image, "rather than

---

73. Rhodes and Tisby, "Black Ministers Release Charlottesville Declaration," para. 8.
74. Evans et al., "Critical Theory."
75. Evans et al., "Critical Theory," para. 2.
76. Evans et al., "Critical Theory," para. 4.

77. Evans et al., "Critical Theory," para. 7. The idea of a racial double standard is a contentious point in this conversation and can be seen in the back-and-forth of these blogs and videos: Tisby and Burns, "Processing Donald Trump"; Alpha & Omega Ministries, "RAAN and 'Feeling Safe'"; Tisby, "Trump's Election and Feeling 'Safe'"; Tisby, "Downside of Integration for Black Christians"; Webb, "Open Reply to Jemar Tisby."

from the contingencies of race, gender, and ethnicity."[78] The doctrine of sin demonstrates that, even though "sinfulness can express itself in different ways depending upon social location," the bottom line is that "all stand in need of God's mercy."[79] The incarnation shows the dignity and unity of humanity.[80] Finally, the doctrines of reconciliation and the church show how unity in Christ breaks down all barriers, providing a more firm foundation for true unity than "the contingent social distinctions of race, gender, and ethnicity."[81] Indeed, this unity in Christ is so precious to reconciliation that it must be protected against the threat of "dubious and irremediably divisive secular theories."[82]

Clearly, there is division concerning the parameters of the discussion. As the CT Statement suggests, the concept of race must be judged theologically, rather than sociologically; one's status in Christ is more real than the mere "contingencies of race . . . and ethnicity."[83] And yet, the Declaration uses theology, drawing on the doctrines of creation and sin to explain the embodied reality of race, with a firm biblical-theological appreciation that "judgment begins with the household of God."[84] Both statements also believe the gospel is the solution to racism. "We declare that old time religion is good enough for us in this new era," claims the Declaration,[85] while the CT Statement places itself in the tradition of Black Presbyterian minister Francis J. Grimke: "I have faith in the power of the religion of the Lord Jesus Christ to conquer all prejudices . . ."[86] Lamentably, these two statements talk past one another, even while using the same biblical and theological tradition and holding to the same belief in the gospel for change.

This trend continues. In 2018, John MacArthur and numerous conservative Reformed pastors published a "Statement on Social Justice and the Gospel," seeking to address racial divisions through theology, rather than "questionable sociological, psychological, and political theories," but this pointed document alienated many within the Reformed and evangelical

---

78. Evans et al., "Critical Theory," para. 6.

79. Evans et al., "Critical Theory," para. 7.

80. Evans et al., "Critical Theory." Interestingly, this point holds promise for both sides. As will be shown, the doctrine of the incarnation indeed holds tremendous promise for reconciliation, as it is upon the flesh of Jesus that various theologians have built powerful arguments for the dignity of oppressed minorities.

81. Evans et al., "Critical Theory," para. 9.

82. Evans et al., "Critical Theory," para. 9.

83. Evans et al., "Critical Theory," para. 6.

84. Rhodes and Tisby, "Black Ministers Release Charlottesville Declaration," para. 3.

85. Rhodes and Tisby, "Black Ministers Release Charlottesville Declaration," para. 5.

86. Evans et al., "Critical Theory," para. 5.

community.[87] In 2021, Duke Kwon and Greg Thompson, both PCA Teaching Elders, published *Reparations: A Christian Call for Repentance and Repair*, which makes thorough use of the concept of White supremacy.[88] Shortly after its publication, Kevin DeYoung, another PCA TE, published a critical review, targeting the use of such language as, at the least, unhelpful, and at worst, unable to capture a genuinely Christian vision of transformation.[89] In response, Kwon and Thompson published a rebuttal, which states that DeYoung's criticism of White supremacy as a concept stems from his own cultural commitments: "While Reverend DeYoung's subtitle indicates that he believes his review to be an expression of a theological project, *we believe his review actually to be expressive of a cultural project that seeks perennially to justify itself on theological grounds*. And that cultural project is, in one inelegant and highly disturbing phrase, *White supremacy*."[90] Clearly, the debate about critical theory is far from settled. If anything, the gulf between different viewpoints has only grown wider.

MINISTRY CHALLENGE: ARE WE WELCOME?

Beneath this technical question about language and terminology lies a cultural divide. Many PCA elders do not currently recognize the White cultural overtones present in the denomination. As Black PCA pastor Mike Higgins states:

> The denomination "does not know what it does not know," when it comes to minority cultures. Minorities in predominantly White "worlds" really don't have any choice but to become cross-cultural if they want to thrive. This means that they have to understand and navigate "Whiteness." However, for the most part, Whites don't have to be cross-cultural; they are dominant. Whites can afford to not know, but minorities must know.[91]

---

87. Buice et al., "Statement on Social Justice & the Gospel," para. 1. For critical engagement with the statement, see: Lee and Lindgren, "John MacArthur's 'Statement on Social Justice,'" and Foley and Hawkins, "Evangelical Response."

88. Kwon and Thompson, *Reparations*, 15.

89. DeYoung, "Reparations." Discussing the book's closing illustration of what a world without White supremacy could look like, DeYoung writes, "the religious vision is still one that I find more in line with a community organizer's dream for America than a distinctively Christian one."

90. Thompson and Kwon, "Sanctifying the Status Quo," para. 9 (italics original).

91. Higgins, "African American Church Planters," 103–4. The perceived normativity of Whiteness that Higgins describes is explored together with the concept of privilege in Moore, "Race," 653–54.

The "Whiteness" that Higgins describes manifests in numerous ways. For instance, as Rev. Baird aptly states, the denomination was started "for the sake of the Scripture, for the sake of the preservation of historic Presbyterianism, and for the furtherance of the gospel proclamation."[92] These points are clearly identifiable in the founding document, "Message to All Churches." They are laudable commitments. Yet, this mission statement is silent on race. For some, historic Presbyterianism looks like White church officers preventing Black Christians from entering worship. How should the PCA reckon with the dissonance between our theological commitments and our cultural heritage? This question, and the many like it, remains unresolved, revealing what is at heart a cultural divide within the PCA.[93]

What is the gospel? What is racism? Why should we focus on race at all? According to some, racial issues are not gospel issues, and thus the church cannot comment on them. Many elders define racism simply as hatred of other races, without making room for a larger definition that includes racial pride or cultural disdain. Many majority-culture elders argue for a color-blind approach to race: ignore race and treat individuals as individuals.

In contrast, the voices of minority elders answer these questions quite differently. They insist that racial reconciliation is integral to gospel faithfulness: "It's not an addition to the gospel, it is a faithful working out of the gospel. Cross-cultural community offers a unique foretaste of the kingdom that is to come."[94] For them, racism is more insidious than mere hate; it is "the unbiblical and ungodly conviction that certain groups of people are not only different, but in some way inferior and less desirable than others, coupled with the conviction that certain other groups are more pure and godly."[95] Finally, they regard "color-blindness" as theologically and intellectually deficient. It fails to take account of the pluriform creativity of God, the impact of culture on one's thinking, and the benefits of being White, in that only White people can actively try to ignore race; for people of color, the reality of race confronts them every day.[96]

These divergent answers explain why Black pastors feel alienated within the denomination. The PCA's majority culture answers significant theological questions in ways that maintain their own comfort and cultural power, to the exclusion of others. If the gospel merely concerns personal

---

92. LeCroy, "Transcript of Rev. Jim Baird's Speech," para. 2.

93. While it is true that there are Whites on either side of this divide, the pressure created by this divide disproportionately affects minorities.

94. Whitfield, "Ferguson and Your Local Church," para. 8.

95. Lewis, "Black Pastoral Leadership and Church Planting," 32.

96. Higgins, "African American Church Planters," 103–4.

salvation, then ethical complaints get ignored, overlooked, or labeled as someone playing the race card. If racism is exclusively hatred of another race, there is no motivation for rooting out preferences that impede racial hospitality. If Christians should ignore race altogether, the White majority remain comfortably unaware of their race, while racial minorities are chastised for a preoccupation with race. Such a church would be notably inhospitable to minorities, even while insisting that its doors are open. Lance Lewis, a Black PCA pastor and church planter, sums up this cultural divide when he writes to White readers: "you just don't know us and we do not trust you."[97]

This tension is evident in the growth of organizations and events led by African American Presbyterians seeking racial reconciliation. The past decade has seen the development of the Reconciliation and Justice Network,[98] Leadership Development Resource conferences,[99] the African American Ministries subcommittee,[100] and the African American Presbyterian Fellowship (AAPF), which exists in part to "help the PCA have a better understanding of African American culture and church."[101] While many majority-culture elders pursue the tactic of "color-blindness," these ministries bring the issue of race to the fore.

Such education is necessary. The expressed preferences of the majority culture implicitly signal that minorities are not fully welcome.[102] An example of implicit exclusion comes from the 2015 GA opening worship service. One portion of the liturgy was dedicated to a congregational prayer, thanking God for the work of previous saints by stating, "we remember our forebears and honor and praise you for the faithful servants who have more recently taught and established us in the faith."[103] The first name on the list was Dr. Morton Smith, the first moderator of the PCA's Assembly, who fought to uphold the spirituality of the church, who said in 2002: "I do not consider myself a racist, because I would define a racist as being one

---

97. Lewis, "Black Pastoral Leadership and Church Planting," 35.
98. Reconciliation and Justice Network, "About."
99. African American Ministries, "LDR."
100. African American Ministries. "About African American Ministries."
101. Plummer, "Introducing the African American Presbyterian Fellowship."

102. This is why the pressure of the cultural divide lands disproportionately on minorities—as a White man, even if I disagree with the dominant historical paradigm, I am not necessarily excluded because of my skin color, whereas minorities must wrestle with the question of being truly welcome at the table as soon as they walk in the door.

103. General Assembly worship service, July 11, 2015, in Chattanooga, Tennessee. Liturgies from previous Assemblies are archived at the PCA Historical Center. My thanks to Wayne Sparkman for his archival assistance.

who hates another race. I personally have no problems with segregation of the races, if it had involved a full equality of practice with the races . . . I do not consider myself a racist, though I have no objection to the segregation of the races."[104] A mere thirteen years after that interview, racial minorities worshiping at GA participated in an unqualified thanks for his ministry. This move was tone-deaf to history and culture, just one more stumbling block for minority pastors to experience a true and full welcome.

Throughout this survey of PCA history, the questions of culture and theology, of race and the gospel, cry out for answers. The testimony of Black brothers and sisters demands that the PCA engage in rigorous introspection: if minorities experience exclusion, is the PCA truly "faithful to the Scriptures, true to the Reformed Faith, and obedient to the Great Commission?"

---

104. P&R News, "Interview with Morton Smith," 15.

2

Outsiders in the Kingdom?

Racial Inclusivity and Biblical Theology

JESUS FAMOUSLY PRAYED IN John 17 that his church would be one. In a world of division, Christian unity witnesses to God's glorious salvation. The North American church has yet to realize the fullness of Jesus' prayer. Its history is marked by borders and boundaries, separating God's people from one another.[1] As Dr. Martin Luther King Jr. once lamented, it is "one of the shameful tragedies [of our nation] that eleven o'clock on Sunday morning is one of the most segregated hours, if not the most segregated hour, in Christian America."[2] For the PCA, this should be a matter of great concern. The denomination's commitment to the Scriptures and to the Great Commission should lead the church toward racial hospitality and ethnic inclusivity. But, to have true reconciliation, we must first understand the biblical dynamics of exclusion and inclusion within God's kingdom. Who is in? Who is out? And can there be outsiders on the inside of God's kingdom?

---

1. This is the history of the slave trade: the wrong boundaries were broken, and the wrong boundaries were enforced. National boundaries were broken as people were stolen from their homeland. The breaking of national boundaries was empowered by prior acceptance of false anthropological boundaries: Africans were deemed less than fully human (anthropological boundary established); therefore, it was proper to enslave them (national boundary broken). Once the anthropological boundary had been drawn, national boundaries could be crossed with impunity. The scars of such violence, to and because of boundaries, have sown generations of hatred and conflict in America. For more on the relationship between the false anthropological boundary empowering the breaking of national boundaries, see Jennings, *Christian Imagination*, esp. 60–203.

2. "Interview on 'Meet the Press,'" para. 54.

EXCLUSION AND INCLUSION IN THE OLD TESTAMENT

Embedded Boundaries: An Ordered Cosmos

Creational Boundaries—Genesis 1

A biblical theology of racial inclusivity begins in Genesis 1. "Genesis itself, explained methodically, encompasses a mirror of all of life . . . whether one wishes to consider divine matters, or politics, or household affairs."[3] The creation narrative in Genesis 1 lays the foundation for any discussion about inclusion and exclusion within the church.

One of the central words describing God's creative activity is בדל, meaning to "separate," or "divide from."[4] Throughout Genesis 1, God draws boundaries in the new creation, dividing light and dark (1:4), heavens and earth (1:6–7), and day and night (1:14, 18).

God's boundary-making then extends intimately into every part of the life that springs forth in this freshly divided space. Every new phase of created life is marked with God's boundaries. All plants, trees, fish, birds, insects, livestock, and other "beasts of the earth" are given the ability to procreate, "each according to its kind" (1:11, 21, 24, 25). This phrase indicates the "distinction of kind," pointing to boundaries drawn within created order.[5] The entire creation, from cosmology to biology, is embedded with God-drawn boundaries, culminating with humanity. Made in God's image as male and female, humanity encapsulates and embodies the creation narrative: God created a perfectly organized world, with God-given boundaries signaling his order.[6]

As the narrative shows, God is happy with this organization. He repeatedly declares his ordered world to be good (1:4, 10, 12, 18, 21, 25, 31). Each instance of boundary-making further distances the creation from its former condition of being "without form and void." The dividing of space and time enables culture and agriculture, "for everything there is a season, and a time for every matter under heaven" (Eccl 3:1), because God organized the cosmos. God's boundary-making transforms a "confused emptiness" into a world that brings forth and sustains life.[7] God's boundaries, therefore, lead to *shalom*: the flourishing of the entirety of creation.[8]

---

3. Pelargus, quoted in Thompson, *Genesis 1–11*, 4.
4. Köhler, *Hebrew and Aramaic Lexicon of the Old Testament*, 1:110.
5. Delitzsch, *New Commentary on Genesis*, 1:90.
6. Waltke and Fredricks, *Genesis*, 66.
7. Calvin, *Genesis*, 1:73.
8. Plantinga, *Not the Way*, 10.

Because of this, Genesis 1 suggests a theme that will be unfolded throughout Scripture. If God's boundaries lead to *shalom*, it is important to respect those boundaries. Obedience leads to peace—peace within creation and peace with God himself.[9] "Boundaries are important in both the creation and social orders. When everything keeps to its allotted place and does not transgress its limits, there is order, not chaos."[10] The creation obeys God's boundaries and experiences *shalom*. In the same way, humanity will be called to obey God's boundaries in order to experience *shalom*. This leads to the ethical boundaries of law.

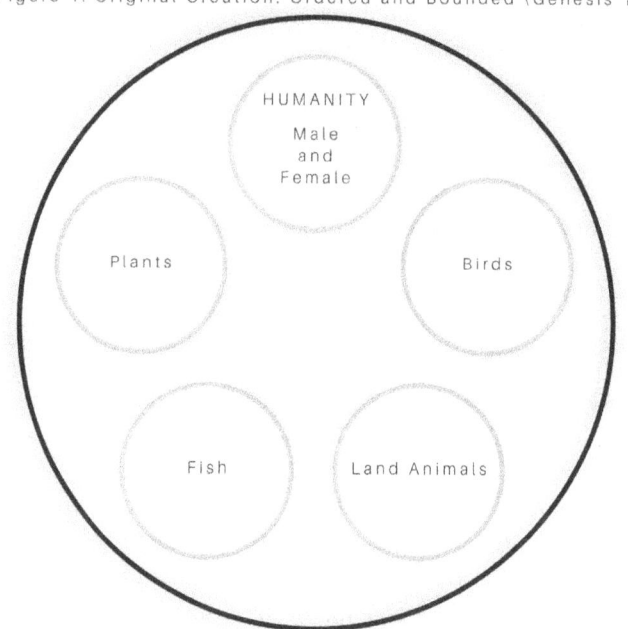

Figure 1: Original Creation: Ordered and Bounded (Genesis 1)

Ethical Boundaries—Genesis 2

God's ethical boundaries are quickly established as the story continues. Thus far, God's commands are permissive: "Let there be." However, in Genesis 2, God's first prohibitive command appears: "Of the tree of the knowledge of good and evil you shall not eat" (2:17). This ethical boundary makes explicit what was implicit before: God requires obedience to his boundaries. This

---

9. Ratzinger, 'In the Beginning,' 15.
10. Waltke and Fredricks, *Genesis*, 56. See also Fig. 1.

behavioral commandment reinforces the fundamental boundary throughout Genesis: God is distinct from humanity, and humanity must keep the law of the King.[11]

Far from being repressive, submission to God's ethical boundaries brings *shalom*. Genesis 1 and 2 portray a God whose special delight rests in his relationship with humanity. Obedience simply meant clinging to God in faithfulness, so that nothing could disrupt the relationship of sustaining love that was present from the beginning. Echoing the creational ordering of Genesis 1, Calvin states that, ethically, "our life will then be rightly ordered, if we obey God."[12] This promise of experiencing *shalom* through obedience enables Christians to declare, in contrast to all cultures of human autonomy, "to serve you is perfect freedom."[13]

However, if obedience to God's ethical boundaries brings *shalom*, transgression brings death: "for in the day that you eat of it you shall surely die" (2:17).[14] Failure to respect God's boundaries ultimately leads to spiritual death, full separation from God.[15] Obedience and disobedience change the tenor of the boundary between God and humanity. Obedient humanity is still distinct from God by virtue of the Creator-creature distinction. Disobedient humanity, on the other hand, is removed from God's presence, and the boundary hardens due to God's judgment. At this point in the story, it remains to be seen whether anything can soften this boundary, such as grace.

Ecclesial Boundaries—Genesis 3

The possibility of judgment in Genesis 2 is realized in Genesis 3. Through the serpent's temptation, Adam and Eve reject and transgress God's boundaries.[16] Death threatens to return the world to chaos, as strife enters every sphere of the created order. God's boundaries harden in judgment and create pain at every level: obedient work becomes toilsome, marital harmony becomes compromised, and fellowship with God becomes impossible.

---

11. Waltke and Fredricks, *Genesis*, 87. See also Psalm 24:1: "The earth is the Lord's and the fullness thereof."

12. Calvin, *Genesis*, 1:126.

13. *Book of Common Prayer*, 99.

14. As Derek Kidner states, "the idea of 'dividing' is specially prominent, both [in Creation] and in the Law. . . since this way lies cosmos . . . and the other way chaos" (Kidner, *Genesis*, 51).

15. Waltke and Fredricks, *Genesis*, 87.

16. Derek Kidner calls this decision "the alternative to discipleship: to be self-made, wresting one's knowledge, satisfactions and values from the created world in defiance of the Creator" (Kidner, *Genesis*, 68).

All is not lost, however. Genesis 3:15 promises a grand champion rising out of the ashes of the fall. This redeemer will ultimately remove the judgment from God's boundaries, restoring *shalom*. To preserve this promise, God forms another boundary within humanity, an ecclesial boundary. God divides the faithful from the unfaithful. This introduces a new dynamic within humanity: a covenant community with insiders and outsiders.[17] Humanity is now "divided into two communities: the elect, who love God, and the reprobate, who love self . . . Each of the characters of Genesis will be either of the seed of the woman that reproduces her spiritual propensity, or of the seed of the Serpent that reproduces his unbelief. The unspoken question to the reader is, 'Whose seed are you?'"[18]

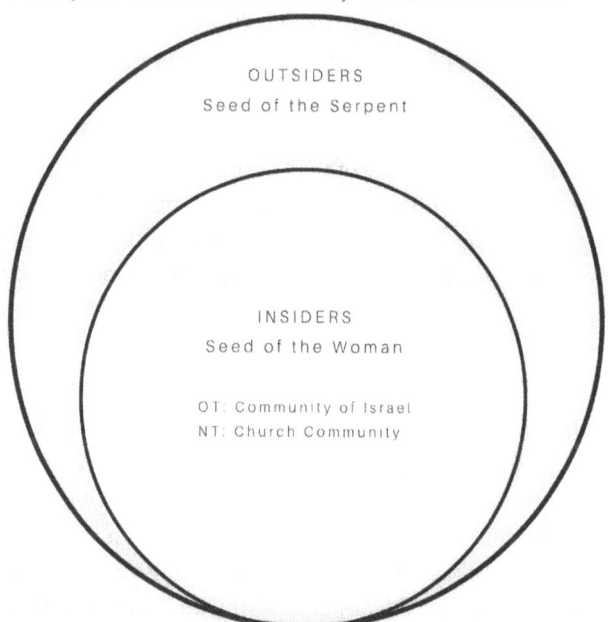

Figure 2: Post-Fall Humanity Divided (Genesis 3)

OUTSIDERS
Seed of the Serpent

INSIDERS
Seed of the Woman

OT: Community of Israel
NT: Church Community

God's ecclesial boundary establishes the trajectory for the rest of the Bible. Genesis outlines the lineages of the godless (the line of Cain) and the godly (the line of Seth), culminating in God preserving Noah's family alone from the flood. After the flood, humanity continues to reject God's authority and rebels against God at Babel. In response, God draws further cultural and national boundaries as an act of discipline. Finally, the ecclesial boundary anchors the story of Abraham, singled out by God to begin the

17. See Figure 2.
18. Waltke and Fredricks, *Genesis*, 94–95.

work of overcoming the boundaries of judgment incurred by the fall: "in you all the families of the earth shall be blessed" (12:3).

Genesis offers a biblical perspective on how God works through boundaries, with four fundamental lessons. First, God is the chief boundary-maker, not humanity. As the Creator, he establishes both creational and ethical boundaries. Second, the purpose of God's boundaries is *shalom*, but obedience is required to experience this *shalom*. When creation obeys his creative word, there is flourishing, and God calls it "very good" (Gen 1:31). When humanity obeys his prescriptive word, there is *shalom*, peace with God and others. Third, transgressing God's boundaries brings judgment. Preexisting boundaries become less about harmonious difference and more about painful division. Fourth, God pursues redemption, drawing an ecclesial boundary within humanity, creating a covenant community to preserve his promises. While primarily exclusive at this stage in the story, this ecclesial boundary foreshadows an inclusive unity: a single people saved by the mysterious champion, the conquering "seed of the woman" with the capacity to unite and bless all nations.

Embodied Boundaries: Election and Law

In Exodus, the boundaries embedded in creation become embodied in God's covenant community. The Exodus narrative provides a dramatic vantage into the missional purpose of God's boundary-making. The promises given to Abraham come to fruition in the community of Israel. Through the boundaries of election and law, they are kingdom insiders, removed from the nations, yet they have a redemptive role to play for the sake of the nations.

Exodus 19:4–6 serves as the galvanizing vision for the covenant community of Israel.[19] God first clarifies the boundary of election. Israel's election is a continuation of God's promises to the patriarchs. They are "the house of Jacob" and "the people of Israel" (19:3), a people set apart for a purpose. God recounts his redemptive actions: "You yourselves have seen what I did to the Egyptians, and how I bore you on eagles' wings and brought you to myself" (19:4). The exodus itself highlights the dual nature of Israel's election: they have been separated from Egypt and separated for the Lord.[20]

This dynamic of negative (chosen from) and positive (chosen for) aspects is clarified as God explains the scope of Israel's election. First, they are God's "treasured possession" (19:5), a phrase that describes Israel as

19. Blackburn, *God Who Makes Himself Known*, 87.
20. See Keil, *Pentateuch*, 1:383.

"valuable property, that which is . . . put aside."[21] Israel's election shows God's tenderness and fatherly care toward his people, as he separates them from the nations. However, there are hints of a larger purpose for their election. God does not simply set his valued possession aside for the sake of hoarding or fear of corruption. Because Israel is set among the nations as God's elect, the "implication is that Israel's status as a treasured possession is . . . also a means to a further end that has in view all peoples of the earth."[22]

After noting their great value to him, the Lord then identifies Israel as a "kingdom of priests" (19:6). This phrase is notable for the variety of possible interpretations, but a strong translation is "priestly kingdom," a nation with a priestly function.[23] As a priestly kingdom, Israel had both a special status and a special purpose because "the priest is set apart by a distinctive way of life consecrated to the service of God and dedicated to ministering to the needs of the people."[24] By setting his people apart as priests who intercede for others, God opens up "the possibility of a relationship between [himself] and the nations," which hints at a future inclusion of the nations into God's people, a salvation accessible to outsiders.[25]

In addition to being a priestly kingdom, they are a "holy nation" (19:6).[26] Throughout the Old Testament, holiness forms Israel's central identity and calling, stemming from God's holiness: "You shall be holy, for I the LORD your God am holy" (Lev 19:2). To be holy was to embody God's character.[27] While a full definition of holiness covers a broad range of meanings, from ethical purity to cultic acceptability to national status, a minimal definition describes both the negative and positive aspects of election: to

21. סגלה; Keil, *Pentateuch*, 1:383.

22. Blackburn, *God Who Makes Himself Known*, 89. This concept of saving aside a special item for a special purpose can be compared to one investing in a luxurious bottle of fine whisky, which is then brought out for special occasions as a blessing to friends and guests.

23. The phrase מַמְלֶכֶת כֹּהֲנִים is challenging in part because it is a *hapax legomenon*, but as Blackburn convincingly argues, it is easily translated in parallel with the following phrase גּוֹי קָדוֹשׁ, "holy nation." Both "nation" and "kingdom" are used synonymously in the OT, and there are strong parallels between "holy" and "priests." Therefore, as קָדוֹשׁ qualifies גּוֹי, interpreted as "holy nation," so כֹּהֲנִים qualifies מַמְלֶכֶת, rendering "priestly kingdom" (See Blackburn, *God Who Makes Himself Known*, 90). Keil, who takes an opposing position, nevertheless states that "there is no essential difference between ['priestly kingdom' and 'royal priesthood'], the kingship being founded upon the priesthood, and the priesthood completed by the kingship" (Keil, *Pentateuch*, 1:385).

24. Sarna, *Exodus*, 104.

25. Blackburn, *God Who Makes Himself Known*, 90.

26. Hebrew: גּוֹי קָדוֹשׁ, another *hapax legomenon* (See Blackburn, *God Who Makes Himself Known*, 92).

27. Keil, *Pentateuch*, 1:385.

be holy is to be "singled out" or "consecrated for" a purpose.[28] Negatively, Israel's holiness marked their being "set apart from others by God by special privilege."[29] Positively, their holiness provided a witness to God's character, and thus "through Israel, God would make himself known to the world."[30]

Israel's election forms an ecclesial boundary with both negative and positive dimensions.[31] This ecclesial boundary was then embodied through the legal boundary, God's law: "if you will indeed obey my voice and keep my covenant, you shall be [my people]" (19:5). Indeed, "obedience to God lies at the heart of the covenant relationship."[32] The clear link between obedience and relationship in Exodus 19, echoing the Genesis account, furthers the negative and positive dimensions of God's boundaries. In the negative sense, the people's adherence to the law embodies their identity as "set apart."[33] As God's distinct community, *shalom* came, not by living like the surrounding nations, but by living in obedience to God's covenant. Positively, the law witnesses to God's character, showing the beauty of the Lord to the nations (cf. Deut 4:6–8). Thus, election and law intertwine to form a distinct boundary between God's people and the surrounding nations with the promise of *shalom*.

These twin mandates of election and law form the ecclesial boundary of God's people, which allows the implications of Genesis 1 to blossom with meaning. In Genesis 1, the word בדל describes God's work of organizing creation by distinguishing each element. In the rest of the OT, the same word describes God's work of distinguishing his people from the rest of the nations. For example, the Levitical law utilizes בדל to command the people to "*distinguish* [לְהַבְדִּיל] between the holy and the common, and between the unclean and the clean" (Lev 10:10; also 11:47 and 20:25) because God had "*separated* [them] [הִבְדַּלְתִּי] from the peoples" (Lev 20:24, 26). This Levitical

---

28. Köhler, *Hebrew and Aramaic Lexicon of the Old Testament*, 3:1066. For a larger discussion of holiness in the Pentateuch, see Hartley, "Holy and Holiness, Clean and Unclean," 420–29.

29. Calvin, *Harmony of Exodus, Leviticus, Numbers, and Deuteronomy*, 2:320.

30. Blackburn, *God Who Makes Himself Known*, 95.

31. Calvin, *Harmony of Exodus, Leviticus, Numbers, and Deuteronomy*, 2:318–20. Calvin references Deuteronomy 32:8–9, which is instructive for viewing the religious and national dimensions of God's election: "When the Most High gave to the nations their inheritance, when he divided mankind, he fixed the borders of the peoples according to the number of the sons of God. But the LORD's portion is his people, Jacob his allotted heritage."

32. Alexander, *From Paradise to the Promised Land*, 177.

33. This supports the centrality of circumcision in the OT. Circumcision, as commanded by God, set one apart from the nations as a member of God's community, which also establishes a robust theology of baptism in the NT.

command to embody their election through a particular lifestyle carries with it the promise of *shalom*. Obedience brings blessing.

Conversely, Israel's failure to obey God's boundaries brings punishment. God indicts Israel for failure to keep his boundaries, making "no *distinction* [הִבְדִּילוּ] between the holy and the common" (Ezek 22:26). This failure led to judgment, a redrawing of the boundaries, so that the insiders are treated as outsiders: "your iniquities have made a *separation* [מַבְדִּלִים] between you and your God, and your sins have hidden his face from you so that he does not hear" (Isa 59:2).

The themes of election and law personalize the boundaries of Genesis 1–3 to God's people. In electing Israel, God shows his authority as Creator and his desire to enjoy communion with the creation. The boundaries of election and law enable Israel to enjoy God's presence and, therefore, his *shalom*. However, they are not simply saved from the world to enjoy God selfishly by excluding others. Rather, their obedience opens the pathway for inclusion as the surrounding nations come to enjoy God through Israel's mission. As Brevard Childs states: "Election by God brings no comfortable special status, but an invitation both to share the redemption of God to the world and to bear witness to his final judgment of sin."[34]

Boundaries as Exclusive and Inclusive: Unidirectional Separation

This inclusive aspect of God's boundary-making raises an important question. If God's people were set apart in order to bless the nations, yet were simultaneously commanded to remain separate from the nations, how could the nations respond in faith? How could gentiles enter the Jewish community to experience fellowship with God? While the OT focuses primarily on Israel's exclusive insider status, there are glimpses of another dimension of this ecclesial boundary: the inclusion of outsiders. Though Israel tended to transgress the boundary of election and law, becoming like the gentiles, there are examples of gentiles passing through the boundary of election and law, becoming like Israel.

The book of Ezra offers a fascinating glimpse into the missionary trajectory of the OT. The theme of renewal is central to Ezra: renewal of the Israelites to Jerusalem, renewal of the temple, renewal of the Passover celebration, and spiritual renewal through repentance.[35] Through this narrative,

---

34. Childs, *Book of Exodus*, 367. Thus, every aspect of Israel's corporate life was revelatory to the surrounding nations, whether in blessing or judgment.

35. Fensham, *Books of Ezra and Nehemiah*, 16–19.

God demonstrates a remarkable flexibility in the use of בדל to reveal both exclusivity and inclusivity in Israel's ecclesial boundary. The negative use occurs in Ezra 9–10, confronting Jews who had taken foreign wives. This intermarriage reflects disregard for God's ecclesial boundary: "The people of Israel and the priests and the Levites have not *separated* [לֹא־נִבְדְּלוּ] themselves from the peoples of the lands with their abominations" (9:1).[36] With the recent experience of exile as punishment for breaking God's boundaries, Ezra leads the people in a covenant renewal ceremony of repentance and recommitment to following the Law. As part of this commitment, the guilty members of the community were called to "*separate* [הִבָּדְלוּ] [them]selves from the peoples of the land and from the foreign wives" (10:11). If they failed to respond to this summons, then they themselves would be "banned [or separated, יִבָּדֵל] from the congregation" (10:8). Ezra reinforces the negative, exclusive OT barrier: Israel is not to cross the ecclesial boundary to join the nations.

However, Ezra also hints that this boundary is semipermeable. Separation is unidirectional. God opens the community boundary to welcome those who want to join in the covenant. Ezra signals this inclusion at one of the central festivals of the Hebrew people: Passover. As part of their spiritual renewal, the postexilic community held Passover, with increased effort to follow God's prescriptions, "as . . . written in the Book of Moses" (6:18), unlike the previous generations. Significantly, amid this pure celebration of Passover, the Jews welcomed "everyone who had joined them and *separated* himself [הַנִּבְדָּל] from the uncleanness of the peoples of the land to worship the LORD, the God of Israel" (Ezra 6:21). This Passover celebration included both ethnic Jews as well as "those with any other background without distinction who joined [the Jews] with wholehearted allegiance."[37] This was not syncretism, but covenant faithfulness: God had always made provision for foreigners to enter the covenant community (cf. Exod 12:44, 48).[38]

Ezra 6 shows how God's grace opens boundaries. The Jews, separated from God because of their sin, were reunited with him through the sacrifices at Passover.[39] At the same time, foreigners were brought into relationship with God, and with God's people, through their own separation "from

---

36. The mention of "their abominations" indicates that far more is at stake here than simply ethnic purity; "the reason . . . had nothing to do with racism, but with a concern for the pure religion of the Lord" (Fensham, *Books of Ezra and Nehemiah*, 124).

37. Williamson, *Ezra, Nehemiah*, 85.

38. Fensham, *Books of Ezra and Nehemiah*, 96.

39. Levering, *Ezra & Nehemiah*, 78. The theme of sacrifice leading to fellowship with God takes on profound implications in the ministry of Jesus, which has important ramifications for the goal of racial reconciliation, to be explored in following chapters.

the uncleanness of the peoples."[40] The boundary separating God's people from the nations was semipermeable. The people of God were prohibited from leaving the covenant community, but the nations could enter through God's grace.[41]

Figure 3: Insiders and Outsiders in the Old Testament

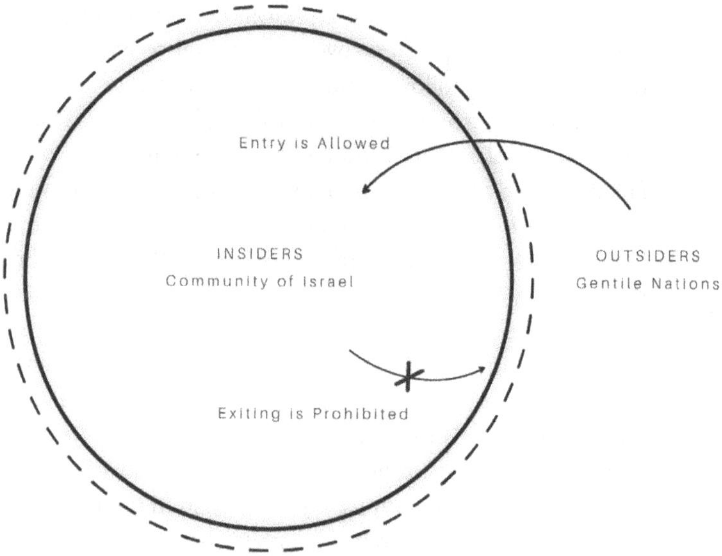

Entry is Allowed

INSIDERS
Community of Israel

OUTSIDERS
Gentile Nations

Exiting is Prohibited

Isaiah 56 also showcases God's grace opening the community boundary. After inviting a rebellious Israel back to himself in chapter 55, God addresses any foreigners who long for inclusion in the covenant community: "Let not the foreigner who has joined himself to the LORD say, 'The LORD will surely *separate* [הַבְדֵּל יַבְדִּילַנִי][42] me from his people'" (Isa 56:3).[43] God demonstrates that his exclusive boundary is also profoundly inclusive; the only entrance requirement is faith:

> "And the foreigners who join themselves to the LORD, to minister to him, to love the name of the LORD, and to be his servants, everyone who keeps the Sabbath and does not profane it, and holds fast my covenant—these I will bring to my holy mountain, and make them joyful in my house of prayer; their burnt

---

40. Williamson, *Ezra, Nehemiah*, 85. Here, again, the focus is on uncleanness, not ethnicity.

41. See Figure 3.

42. An intensifying infinitive of the root בדל; Williams, *Williams' Hebrew Syntax*, 85.

43. Delitzsch, *Isaiah*, 7:537.

offerings and their sacrifices will be accepted on my altar; for my house shall be called a house of prayer for all peoples." The Lord GOD, who gathers the outcasts of Israel, declares, "I will gather yet others to him besides those already gathered." (Isa 56:6–8)

Hints of such a radical inclusion are found throughout the OT, with notable figures like Rahab the Canaanite prostitute (Josh 6:17), Ruth the Moabite (Ruth 1:4), the widow of Zarephath (1 Kgs 17:9), and Naaman the Syrian leper (2 Kgs 5:17) entering into God's people in a redemptive way. These four examples demonstrate God's desire to include outsiders into his people, and they foreshadow an even greater inclusion, prophesied by Isaiah. Such a massive inclusion of gentiles into God's people awaited fulfillment in the New Testament. There, those who gather in the Lord's house of prayer will at last enjoy full insider status, regardless of nationality, ethnicity, or race; as beneficiaries of the final sacrifice for sins, they will be cleansed, forgiven, and restored to fellowship for all time.[44]

Learning from the Old Testament

Throughout the OT, God establishes boundaries that allow humanity to flourish. God's people must respect those boundaries to enjoy and extend God's *shalom*. Election separates God's people from the nations, and the law reinforces that community boundary. Inside this boundary, they enjoy God's presence; in crossing the boundary, they incur God's discipline. However, they are not called merely to enjoy God's presence while disregarding their foreign neighbors. Their faithfulness was an invitation for the nations to come into relationship with God (cf. Ps 2:10–12). Because God desires the worship of all nations, his ecclesial boundary is semipermeable. Separation is only unidirectional—the possibility of outsiders becoming insiders remains. Admittedly, this potential remains more of a possibility than a reality; the OT closes with unfulfilled expectations regarding the nations, hinting that the ministry of the Messiah will include more than national redemption for Israel.

To invoke a metaphor, think of a city with clearly defined borders.[45] These borders define who is a citizen and who is not. In the OT, the city borders consisted of both ethnicity and belief, the long-standing ecclesial boundaries of election and law. The borders clearly marked the people of Israel as God's kingdom citizens. Generally, the gentiles were considered

44. Motyer, *Prophecy of Isaiah*, 467.
45. For an innovative use of city as an image for God's people throughout the Bible, see Alexander, *City of God*.

outsiders, excluded by the city boundaries. However, these boundaries were not impenetrable. God allowed gentiles to become citizens in his city and told of a future day when the city lines would expand to include many more outsiders. This final note, while primarily implicit throughout the OT, becomes explicit in the NT. God's kingdom expansion forms a central focus of Christ's ministry, and sets the stage for a biblical theology of racial inclusion in the church.

EXCLUSION AND INCLUSION IN THE NEW TESTAMENT

Confronting Boundaries: Jesus' Life and Ministry

The New Testament wastes no time in bringing inclusion of outsiders to the fore. Matthew's Gospel opens by declaring that Jesus is the Messiah and the rightful heir to David's throne (1:1). Yet Matthew goes out of his way to show the inclusion of the nations in Jesus' lineage. In one verse (1:5), Matthew includes two of the most explicit examples of gentiles included in God's people—Rahab and Ruth; of the four women mentioned by name, two are clearly gentiles.[46] Moreover, in Matthew's Gospel, the first worshipers of Jesus were gentiles (2:2, 11). The Gospel of John reinforces this aspect of Jesus' mission, with John the Baptist heralding Jesus as "the Lamb of God, who takes away the sin of the world!" (John 1:29). The Gospel writers frequently show Jesus confronting a common misconception of his day, that God intended his boundaries to exclude outsiders.

Yet, even as he challenged the status quo, Jesus stands in continuity with the OT view of ecclesial boundaries. Brevard Childs corrects those who drive a wedge between the two testaments: "The new covenant is not a substitution of a friendly God for the terror of Sinai, but rather a gracious message of an open access to the same God whose presence still calls forth awe and reverence."[47] If this is the case, we can learn by asking how Jesus approached boundaries: How did Jesus navigate the semipermeable boundary surrounding God's people?

Jesus' entire life and ministry shows his desire to empower insiders to remain faithful (exclusivity), while enabling outsiders to become insiders

---

46. It is possible that all four women are gentiles. Some scholars believe Tamar, mentioned in 1:3, was also a foreigner, a Canaanite; similarly, Bathsheba, who is implied in 1:6, might also be a foreigner, as she was married to a Hittite (See France, *Matthew*, 79).

47. Childs, *Book of Exodus*, 384.

(inclusivity). The Gospels highlight exclusivity—Jesus is commited to the distinctiveness of the covenant community. But they also highlight inclusivity—Jesus knows the gentiles are invited into the covenant community. Even in Jesus' first sermons and signs, the Gospels demonstrate his approach to this dual aspect of God's covenantal boundaries.

Jesus enforces the covenant's exclusive boundary by calling his followers to maintain a lifestyle of holiness. Matthew and Mark record Jesus' first official teaching as a call to repentance (Matt 4:17; Mark 1:15). This call to repentance "echoes the Old Testament prophets' frequent summons to Israel to 'return' to God, to abandon their rebellion and come back into covenant-obedience."[48] Because this call to repent is "a call to renew sonship," it is anything but oppressive.[49] In continuity with the OT, these boundaries establish a proper relationship with God, enabling *shalom*. This relationship requires being distinct from the world, as embodied in the OT ideals of holiness, but it leads to flourishing. It is an invitation to truly live (cf. Deut 30:19). Jesus follows up the call to repentance with the Sermon on the Mount, which codifies his kingdom's ethic, further establishing his commitment to ethical exclusivity.[50]

While Jesus upholds the ethical boundary between God's covenant community and the watching world, he relativizes ethnicity, emphasizing the inclusivity of the kingdom. By stressing personal holiness while relativizing ethnicity, Jesus directly confronts the widespread ethnic exclusivism of the first-century Jewish community. Luke records Jesus' first sermon in Nazareth as an exposition of Isaiah 61 (Luke 4:16–30). Jesus' authoritative teaching rivets the locals, but after he applies the words of Isaiah to himself, their hearts are hardened.[51] Anticipating their rejection, Jesus warns them to not simply rest on their Jewish credentials, because God has a practice of seeking out the gentiles when his own people reject him. As evidence, Jesus references two of the clear OT instances of kingdom inclusivity: the widow of Zarephath and Naaman of Syria (4:25–27). In using these examples, Jesus simultaneously demonstrates God's judgment on the Jews for rejecting him and God's desire to include gentiles in his covenant community.[52] The crowd

---

48. France, *Matthew*, 95. See also Lane, *Gospel According to Mark*, 49–51, 65–66.

49. Lane, *Gospel According to Mark*, 50.

50. Here, Jesus illuminates the OT holiness code, showing how outward behavior must be connected with inward obedience, and heightens the call to inward obedience: "Jesus' radical ethic takes its starting-point from the Old Testament law, but does not so much either confirm or abrogate it as transcend it" (France, *Matthew*, 124).

51. Geldenhuys, *Commentary on the Gospel of Luke*, 168.

52. Morris, *Luke*, 128.

in Nazareth understands both implications, but instead of being convicted at the indictment, they reject Jesus' ministry and seek to kill him.

The Gospel of John begins the narrative of Jesus' ministry not with a sermon, but with a sign—Jesus turns water into wine (John 2:1–11). This familiar story sets up Jesus as the fulfillment of OT messianic prophecy: an abundance of wine accompanies God's Messiah.[53] This messianic prophecy includes gentile inclusion (see Isa 56), so the boundary forged by the law of Moses is brought to completion in the person of Christ.[54] Jesus' first sign establishes him as one with authority to open the ecclesial borders of Israel, putting him into direct conflict with the Jewish leadership as he moves from wedding to temple (John 2:13–22).

The overarching theme of this second narrative, the cleansing of the temple, is that the Jews have turned God's life-giving covenant into an exclusive ritualistic boundary. Jesus is irate that the Jews disrespect the temple by making his "Father's house a house of trade" (2:16). This disrespect also led to disdain for the gentiles: the business affairs were taking place in the Court of the Gentiles.[55] Jesus knew the temple was to be "a house of prayer for all the nations" (Mark 11:17). In taking up space for business, the traders prevented the gentiles from drawing near to God for worship.[56] By cleansing the temple, Jesus makes a way for the gentiles to enter, upholding the inclusive invitation of God's kingdom. Therefore, "the Miracle of Cana and the Cleansing of the Temple . . . signify the same fundamental truth: that Christ has come to inaugurate a new order in religion."[57] This new order clearly involves ethnic inclusivity.

Jesus' interaction with the religious leaders introduces a new principle regarding God's boundaries. If God brings judgment when people break his boundaries, he also brings judgment when people invent newer, more exclusive boundaries. Jesus routinely rebukes the religious leadership for setting up boundaries that God did not make. They failed to honor the semipermeable nature of the covenant and hardened the boundary to simply exclude. They block the gentiles from God's house (Mark 11:15–19). They demand adherence to minute legal details, breaking "the commandment of God for the sake of [their] tradition" (Matt 15:3–9). They "shut the kingdom of heaven in people's faces" (Matt 23:13–15). God judged them for creating and adopting human-made, restrictive boundaries that excluded the gentiles.

---

53. Kruse, *John*, 96–97.
54. Bruner, Gospel of John, 139.
55. Kruse, *John*, 101; Bruner, *Gospel of John*, 143.
56. Lane, *Gospel According to Mark*, 406.
57. Dodd, quoted in Bruner, *Gospel of John*, 125.

In contrast, Jesus consistently welcomed gentiles. He talked with a Samaritan woman (4:1–42); he extolled the faith of a Canaanite woman (Matt 16:28) and a Roman centurion (Matt 8:10). His coming was manifestly "a light for revelation to the Gentiles" (Luke 2:32). In doing so, Jesus becomes the gatekeeper to the semipermeable boundary surrounding God's people. Jesus makes an inclusive and exclusive call. He calls all nations to enter God's holiness through him. This is the thrust of the Great Commission. Jesus himself is the door through which the nations can become kingdom insiders.

Overcoming Boundaries: Reconciliation in Real Time

Jesus explicitly opened the door for individuals of any ethnic background to come into his kingdom. However, such a radical change in the ethnic makeup of God's people took years to implement. Church history shows how hard it is to maneuver the racial inclusivity of Jesus' ministry into a racially inclusive church community. The remainder of the NT offers the church a much-needed apostolic word: the church must put her new identity into practice.

In step with the Great Commission, the book of Acts recounts the progress of the gospel "in Jerusalem and in all Judea and Samaria, and to the ends of the earth" (1:8). Acts 2–8 shows the apostles' evangelistic activity in the first three geographic zones. Philip's evangelistic encounter with the Ethiopian eunuch in Acts 8:26–40 is a foretaste of the expansion of the kingdom to the ends of the earth, which begins in earnest in Acts 10. Luke Timothy Johnson dramatically summarizes the tectonic shift that takes place when Cornelius, the gentile, converts:

> Luke has shown his reader how the good news spread . . . reaching in the evangelization of the detested Samaritans and the sexually mutilated Ethiopian those who would be considered at best marginally Jewish by the strict standards of the Pharisees. . . . Now at last Luke is ready to show how the church made this most fundamental and dangerous step, which would involve the greatest struggle and . . . which in fact would in principle establish its identity as a universal and not simply ethnic religion.[58]

God is the initiator in Acts 10, showing his desire to include the gentiles in his kingdom. God sends an angel to Cornelius (10:3), who is commanded to search out the apostle Peter. Peter, meanwhile, receives his

---

58. Johnson, *Acts of the Apostles*, 187.

own heavenly vision, foreshadowing Cornelius's conversion and detailing the heart of the NT semipermeable covenant boundary: "What God has made clean, do not call common" (10:15). The phrase is repeated three times "to show the divine initiative overcoming human resistance."[59] Peter is then commanded by the Spirit to receive Cornelius's visitors without "hesitation" (διακρινόμενος, 10:20). Interestingly, there is a double meaning in διακρινόμενος. In addition to "hesitation," this phrase also means "discrimination."[60] Peter is told to receive the gentile visitors without hesitation or discrimination. Yet again, God is the only one with the authority to make boundaries between the peoples.

After hearing about Cornelius's angelic visitation, Peter's eyes are opened to God's desire for a multiethnic church: "God shows no partiality, but in every nation anyone who fears him and does what is right is acceptable to him" (10:34–35). Such kingdom inclusivity comes about because of the cross: "on the basis of [Jesus'] death and resurrection the Gospel is offered to all people who are willing to receive it and recognize their need of it."[61] Jesus empowers a universal offer of salvation, so Peter can freely proclaim that "everyone who believes in him receives forgiveness of sins through his name" (10:43). God confirms this message by pouring the Spirit out upon everyone present. This further stretched the paradigm of the Jewish Christians, who "were amazed, because the gift of the Holy Spirit was poured out even on the gentiles" (10:45). Everyone present experienced "the grace that crosses boundaries and makes them obsolete."[62] The inclusivity of the kingdom was becoming a bit clearer.

The rest of Acts further depicts the borders of the church growing through ethnic inclusivity. In continuity with the OT, the residents inside the border are those who trust in God's Messiah, while the cross of Christ now enables all nations to come into this believing community. The border remains semipermeable: insiders are called to respect the boundary through holiness; outsiders are invited in through repentance and faith.[63]

---

59. Johnson, *Acts of the Apostles*, 185.
60. Johnson, *Acts of the Apostles*, 185.
61. Marshall, *Acts*, 201.
62. Johnson, *Message of Acts*, 123–24.
63. See Figure 4.

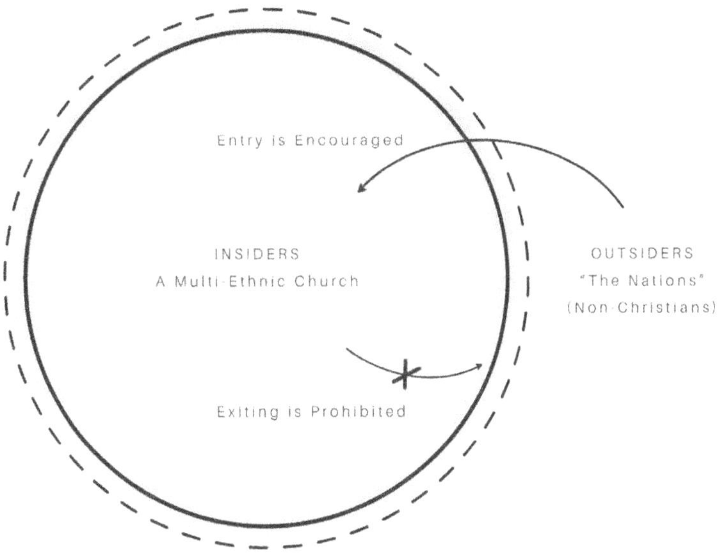

Figure 4: Insiders and Outsiders in the New Testament

Entry is Encouraged

INSIDERS
A Multi-Ethnic Church

OUTSIDERS
"The Nations"
(Non-Christians)

Exiting is Prohibited

This raises a second issue for racial hospitality: church unity. It is one thing to acknowledge that a person of a different ethnicity is a Christian. It is another to embrace them as such. Just as Christ has opened the boundaries around the church, Christ confronts any boundaries within the church. The church must embody Jesus' kingdom-inclusivity within the community. In short, there are to be no outsiders inside the church. In Christ, all Christians are kingdom insiders.

The book of Galatians offers a unique perspective on how Christ's work overcomes any boundaries that remain inside the church. Galatians engages those who demand adherence to the Mosaic law for salvation, specifically requiring the outward sign of circumcision (cf. Gal 5:6).[64] Paul's chief argument throughout the letter is that faith in Christ makes one a true offspring of Abraham, and thus a child in the household of God (3:29).[65] According to Paul, those who demand circumcision for salvation have misunderstood redemptive history: faith in the crucified Christ, not circumcision, brings one into fellowship with God.[66]

64. McKnight, *Galatians*, 23.
65. Hays, *From Every People and Nation*, 183.
66. Additionally, Paul sees a redemptive-historical shift taking place as the sacramental system of Israel becomes reoriented around the person of Christ; from this he argues that baptism replaces circumcision as the mark of covenantal initiation (see esp. 3:27). The "mark of the covenant" receives a new anchor in redemptive history: Jesus' death and resurrection.

Because Jesus opens the boundary to God's people, all ethnicities have equal access to God: "for in Christ Jesus you are all sons of God, through faith. For as many of you as were baptized into Christ have put on Christ. There is neither Jew nor Greek, there is neither slave nor free, there is no male and female, for you are all one in Christ Jesus" (Gal 3:26–28). Church unity, then, is a consequence of the cross. Through his crucifixion, Jesus abolishes all internal boundaries in the covenant community: "whatever may have been their former differences, Christ alone is able to unite them all . . . the distinction is now removed."[67] This new unity is then empowered by the Spirit, who sets in motion Christ's uniting work within the community (Gal 3:2–5). Within the covenant community, human divisions have been overcome in Christ's crucifixion, and through the Spirit, the church is now the new humanity of God, possessing a Spirit-empowered inclusivity.

Christians are called to live out this unity actively, practicing their oneness in Christ in real time. Throughout the NT, the biblical writers appeal for unity in the church (e.g. 1 Cor 10:16–17; Rom 12:4–5; 1 Cor 12:12–13; Col 3:11; Eph 4:4–6; 1 John 4:20–21). Of these texts, Ephesians 2 provides the longest meditation on the practice of reconciliation. Ephesians 2:11–22 applies God's Trinitarian work of atonement to actual church community. Paul argues that reconciliation within the church necessarily accompanies the reconciliation believers have with God through Christ.[68]

Christ's death on the cross kills human-made boundaries between church members: "For he himself is our peace" (Eph 2:14). The crucifixion brought to completion the Mosaic law, previously a "dividing wall of hostility" between Jew and gentile (2:14–15), bringing peace.[69] This peace fulfills God's promises for *shalom*, including interpersonal accord among the covenant community. Through Christ, the horizons of this interpersonal accord expand globally. All Christians are included, "whatever may have been their divisions of race, color, class or creed before."[70] Having ended hostility between peoples inside the church, Christ reconciles the unified church to God through the cross, "thereby killing the hostility" (2:16). Christ's death brings total, comprehensive reconciliation.[71]

After death comes life. The destruction of boundaries births a new community in Christ. Christ's atonement ends with an ethnically and

---

67. Calvin, *Galatians*, 21:112.
68. Foulkes, *Ephesians*, 86–96.
69. Foulkes, *Ephesians*, 90.
70. Foulkes, *Ephesians*, 89.
71. Hays, *From Every People and Nation*, 190.

racially integrated church.⁷² Indeed, "in Christ, there is a new humanity; and it is a single entity."⁷³ Here, too, the Spirit actuates the reconciling work of Christ within this new community (2:18, 22). The ongoing mandate for believers is "to maintain the unity of the Spirit in the bond of peace" (Eph 4:3). Therefore, biblical reconciliation involves actively embracing Christ's new community as the Spirit continues to destroy internal boundaries inside the church. By striving for oneness in the power of the Spirit, the church grows to embody the radical gospel unity envisioned in Gal 3:28.⁷⁴

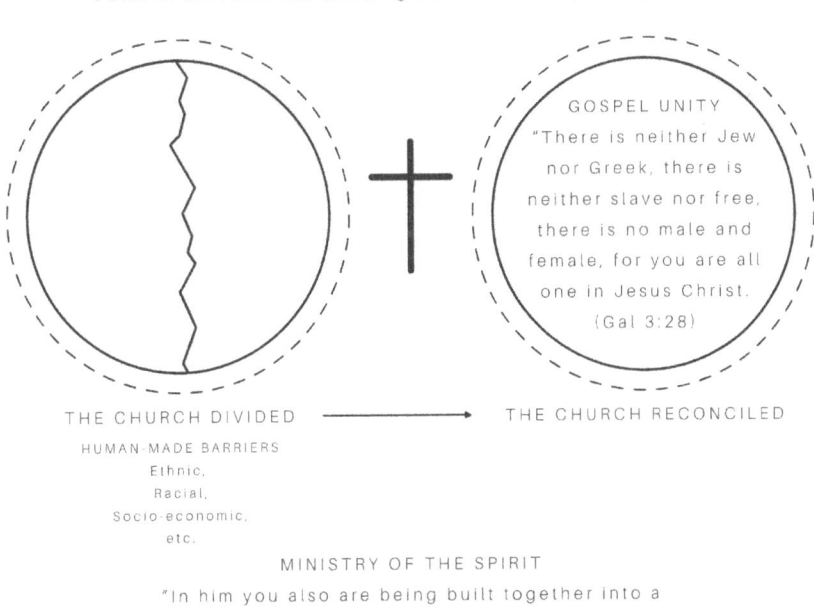

Figure 5: Biblical Reconciliation: Erasing Pre-existing Exclusionary Boundaries and Embracing New Life in the Spirit

---

72. "Gentiles do not simply rise to the status of Jews, but both become something new and greater" (Foulkes, *Ephesians*, 91).

73. Foulkes, *Ephesians*, 90

74. Hays, *From Every People and Nation*, 190. See Figure 5.

The Spirit applies the reconciliation of Christ to every anthropological division within the church.[75] Paul's letter to Philemon envisions reconciliation between slave and free. James applies the gospel to overcome barriers between rich and poor (Jas 2:1–4). Likewise, Paul appeals to the unity of the church to include Christians left out of community practices (1 Cor 11:18–22). Class and socioeconomic distinctions are out of place in Christ's unified body, so Paul instructs believers to "live in harmony with one another. Do not be haughty, but associate with the lowly" (Rom 12:16).

Similarly, racial, ethnic, and regional divisions are out of place in this reconciled body: "Here there is not Greek and Jew, circumcised and uncircumcised, barbarian, Scythian, slave, free; but Christ is all, and in all" (Col 3:11). John the apostle experiences a stunning vision of this reconciled community: "a great multitude that no one could number, from every nation, from all tribes and peoples and languages, standing before the throne and before the Lamb, clothed in white robes, with palm branches in their hands, and crying out with a loud voice, 'Salvation belongs to our God who sits on the throne, and to the Lamb!'"(Rev 7:9–10). Christ will bring this work of reconciliation to completion in the new heaven and Earth, giving humanity access to the Tree of Life, whose "leaves were for the healing of the nations" (Rev 22:2). On that great day, the great chasm rent in humanity through the fall will be fully repaired through the work of Christ. All who were previously outsiders are now insiders, embracing each other as mutual insiders, equal kingdom citizens through the work of the Lamb.

Learning from the New Testament

With this climactic ending, the NT completes the kingdom portrait envisioned in Genesis: one multinational and multiethnic people of God.[76] The person and work of Jesus Christ expands the boundary around God's people, including the nations formerly considered outsiders. This boundary retains its semipermeable character; insiders are those who trust in Christ and are called to lives of holiness, while outsiders are invited into the community by placing their faith in Christ.

In continuity with the OT vision of God's boundaries bringing *shalom*, Jesus' ecclesial boundary is life-giving. Reconciliation with God through Christ brings true life (John 14:6; cf. Col 3:3). This new life brings peace into the community of believers, who are made one despite ethnic, racial, or socioeconomic distinctions (Eph 2:11–22). The life-giving *shalom* of Christ

---

75. Hays, *From Every People and Nation*, 199–200.
76. Hays, *From Every People and Nation*, 205.

comes through the life-giving Spirit (Gal 3:2–3; Eph 2:22). As with the OT, this *shalom* cannot be hoarded inside the community. Jesus connects *shalom* within the church with his mission to the world (John 17:20–23); as Christians embody God's *shalom*, the nations (those who do not trust in Christ) are drawn in and invited to enter the community as well. In this way, Christ's healing expands outwardly into the world, dismantling human-made borders and boundaries in its wake.

Because of this, the NT requires ethnic and racial reconciliation in the church as response to the kingdom's semipermeable boundaries.[77] Christian unity is, therefore, both exclusive and inclusive. The church is distinctly different from a racially fractured world. Christians' greatest identity marker is their union with Christ, not any human-made boundary markers. But true unity remains racially diverse. The nations are invited into the church, bringing their distinctive glory (see Rev 21:24).

This leads to a robust ethic of Christocentric reconciliation. Because Christ tore down the walls of hostility between God and the church, and between Jew and gentile, the church is called to tear down any remaining anthropological boundaries that prevent lived-out Christian unity. Christians must embrace this new life together in the Spirit. As the example of the Pharisees demonstrates, God brings judgment on those who knowingly erect unsanctioned boundaries. By making unsanctioned boundaries, humans ultimately fail to respect God's exclusive authority to draw and maintain boundaries, a lesson as old as Genesis 1. Therefore, Christocentric reconciliation is part of the church's mission and part of her faithfulness. Through proper stewardship of God's boundaries, Christians of all races find *shalom*, true life with God and his people.

To extend the metaphor of the kingdom as God's city: if the original city lines surrounding the OT community tentatively welcomed outsiders in, Jesus expanded the city lines to explicitly include the outsider gentiles into God's newly enlarged city. As with all border expansions, there are growing pains. On paper, previous lines are easily erased and new lines established. But in practice, it takes a while for the previous divisions to disappear, for the newly incorporated insiders to feel like true community insiders. If discipleship is having Christ fully formed in the church (Gal 4:19), part of discipleship is the pursuit of racial inclusivity. This takes place through the power of Christ's Spirit, so that there remain no outsiders on the inside of the church.

---

77. Hays, *From Every People and Nation*, 204–5.

CONCLUSION: TOWARD BIBLICAL RACIAL INCLUSIVITY

The Bible tells the story of God's redemption of the cosmos, his well-sorted and bounded creation. At the center of this story stand a cross and an empty tomb. Jesus reunites humanity in himself, in order to reunite humanity to God, overcoming the boundaries of judgment and division. God's people must live into the shape of this redemptive story—outsiders have become insiders through the work of Christ. In a world marred by human rebellion—disregarding God's ordained creational boundaries and erecting harmful human-made boundaries—the church is a witness to God's reconciling work. Our friendships, our congregations, our ministry, and our hospitality are a demonstration that, in this fractured world, the triune God intends to bring peace. There are no outsiders in the kingdom: all Christians must be welcomed as insiders. For the PCA to be fully faithful to the Scriptures and fully obedient to the Great Commission, there must be no Christians left as outsiders within our churches.

3

Why Diversity?

A Reformed Theology of Church Diversity

IN MODERN US CULTURE, diversity is the watchword. From coffee shops and local bookstores, to fitness centers and libraries, to major international corporations, organizations across the nation trumpet a commitment to diversity. This is far from a merely secular value, however. Diversity is a distinctly Christian virtue. As shown in the previous chapter, the Bible prizes diversity. But Christian leaders wishing to cultivate diversity often face challenges from the pews. Many Christians view a push for diversity with skepticism, so church leaders need compelling answers to this common question: "Why diversity?"

The biblical storyline itself provides the basic answer. But, as history has shown, leaders can also misuse the Scriptures to achieve their own personal ends, so it becomes important to read the Bible along the grain of church tradition. Doctrine helps keep exegesis honest. Especially when facing such a deeply rooted challenge as racial diversity, churches must mine the tradition for resources. Since PCA pastors are committed to being "true to the Reformed faith," it is necessary to reflect on the following question: How does the Reformed tradition help address diversity? For this task, we turn to one of the greatest theologians in the Reformed tradition to develop a doctrine for diversity.

Herman Bavinck's theology of diversity offers profound insight for those seeking a doctrinal imperative for racial diversity. This is particularly beneficial for current discussions within the PCA.[1] For all the thought put into a biblical theology of diversity, there has not been a corresponding amount of attention given to systematics. Many pastors use the Bible to develop a philosophy of ministry that includes diversity, but simply prooftext their claims without connecting diversity to the deeper theological themes of the tradition.[2] We need deeper reflection on church tradition, connecting God's redemptive mission to the nations with the local neighborhood parish.

Though Bavinck wrote over a century ago, his thinking offers a strong foundation for our time. Bavinck wrote during the peak of the modern philosophical movement in the Netherlands.[3] According to Bavinck, modernity was caught between an overemphasis on the individual and an overemphasis on the community.[4] He believed the Reformed tradition offered balance between these two impulses. Prioritizing the individual led to chaotic diversity. Prioritizing the community led to uniformity. Instead, Bavinck prized unity-in-diversity.[5] With this conviction, Bavinck sought to position unity-in-diversity within the heart of Reformed dogmatics.[6] By rooting diversity in systematic theology, we can freshly apply Bavinck's

---

1. Shortly before the 2016 GA, there was a flurry of writing to aid church leaders in thinking through racial diversity in preparation for General Assembly voting. For example, thirty PCA elders published a book encouraging repentance, reconciliation, and diversity. At the same time, the denomination's magazine, *byFaith*, published a steady stream of articles concerning diversity. See Serven et al., *Heal Us, Emmanuel*; Fikse, "Diversity for the Sake of the Gospel"; and Fowler, "Diversity Dance."

2. Such prooftexting opens the door to larger problems. Without a robust biblical and theological framework for diversity, the concept takes on whatever definition is culturally popular. Some might take the push for diversity beyond the limits of Scripture, pushing for every manner of diversity to be accepted within the church. Others will believe that any call for diversity is simply cultural captivity, and resist it at all costs. Finally, unless there is greater support from the Reformed tradition, the cost of diversity becomes hard to justify with simple prooftexts. For example, the popular pastoral vision of having a local congregation embody the diversity of a local neighborhood is exemplified in the articles "Diversity for the Sake of the Gospel" and "The Diversity Dance," with little systematic theological justification. While I celebrate the impulse of these articles, my pastoral concern is that without doctrinal support, these assertions put pressure on young pastors to adopt an agenda for their churches with few theological resources to support that vision. Depending on the neighborhood, this goal could require intensive language training for pastors, provisions for multilingual preaching, hiring multiethnic staff, and learning multilingual songs. Simply invoking a few Bible verses will not easily convince skeptics that such an outpouring of resources is a missional imperative. Such controversy could lead to pastoral burnout or congregational division.

3. Bolt, "Editor's Introduction," 13.

4. Philosophical monism in the academy provided fuel for an overemphasis on the individual, while the socialist political movement created the overemphasis on community.

5. See, for instance, Eglinton, *Trinity and Organism*, 67–71.

6. Eglinton, *Trinity and Organism*, 25–26.

insights to the current question of racial diversity, offering a clear call to pursue diversity for God's glory.

Bavinck's theology provides three necessary components to a doctrine of racial diversity. The first component is protology, God's original plan for a diverse creation. The second component is eschatology, God's victory in Christ securing a diverse future. The final component is ecclesiology, God's redeemed, diverse church in the present. The church's unity and catholicity provide an ethical mandate to pursue diversity in the local, visible church.

FIRST THINGS: DIVERSITY IN BAVINCK'S DOCTRINE OF CREATION

"In the beginning, God created . . ." (Gen 1:1)

Bavinck roots his theology of creation in his doctrine of God. The Trinity is the mold for all creation: everything bears the imprint and reflection of God, the Three-in-One.[7] Following Nicene orthodoxy, Bavinck stresses the unity of the Godhead; "there is in God but one eternal, omnipotent, and omniscient being, having one mind, one will, and one power."[8] This emphasis on unity does not, however, preclude diversity.[9] Quite the opposite: the grandness of God consists in his "absolute unity as well as absolute diversity."[10] God's unity-in-diversity demonstrates the "fullness of being, the true life, eternal beauty."[11] The Trinity is the pinnacle of all things good, true, and beautiful, completely worthy of praise precisely because of God's unity and diversity.[12]

Because the Creator is gloriously unified and diverse, his creation reflects these attributes: "Just as God is one in essence and distinct in persons, so also the work of creation is one and undivided, while in its unity it is still

---

7. Eglinton, *Trinity and Organism*, xi.

8. Bavinck, *Reformed Dogmatics: God and Creation*, 300.

9. "The glory of the confession of the Trinity consists above all in the fact that that unity, however absolute, does not exclude, but includes diversity. God's being is not an abstract unity or concept, but a fullness of being, an infinite abundance of life, whose diversity, so far from diminishing the unity, unfolds it to its fullest extent" (Bavinck, *Reformed Dogmatics: God and Creation*, 300). Throughout Bavinck's corpus, fullness and diversity belong together; clearly Bavinck's view of God and creation is one of abundance.

10. Bavinck, *Reformed Dogmatics: God and Creation*, 332.

11. Bavinck, *Reformed Dogmatics: God and Creation*, 331.

12. See Bavinck's article, "On Beauty and Aesthetics," for a description of God as the basis for these classical transcendentals in *Essays on Religion, Science, and Society*, 255.

rich in diversity."[13] Reflecting God's being, unity and diversity in creation are complementary attributes: "Here is a unity that does not destroy but rather maintains diversity, and a diversity that does not come at the expense of unity, but rather unfolds it in its riches."[14]

The unity-in-diversity of creation is not an obscure footnote in God's design. For Bavinck, it is the only acceptable interpretation of the Scriptures throughout church history.[15] Put succinctly, "this [doctrine of creation] is *the* Christian worldview."[16] Creation's unity-in-diversity explains the beauty of nature.[17] It argues against anti-Christian philosophies.[18] It corrects non-Christian religions.[19] And, it issues in the delight of humanity and the glory of God.[20]

This creational logic extends to humanity: like God, and like the rest of creation, humanity is a glorious unity-in-diversity. In fact, humanity is the fullest demonstration of God's unity-in-diversity by nature of possessing God's image.[21] As made in God's image, humanity is male and female (Gen 1:27; 2:23). This original diversity is more than simply sexual differentiation; it explains the full diversity of humanity rooted in the physical body.[22] The

---

13. Bavinck, *Reformed Dogmatics: God and Creation*, 422.

14. Bavinck, *Reformed Dogmatics: God and Creation*, 436. Note that in describing both God and creation, Bavinck explains that diversity has a role in "unfolding" unity, in a way that brings out its abiding abundance.

15. To support his argument at this section, Bavinck's references include Athanasius, Pseudo-Dionysius, Aquinas, Calvin, Zanchius, and an extended meditation on Augustine (Bavinck, *Reformed Dogmatics: God and Creation*, 436–38).

16. Bavinck, *Reformed Dogmatics: Abridged in One Volume*, 274 (emphasis original). John Bolt, editor of the four-volume full translation, edited this abridged version of the Dogmatics. As such, the abridgments offer something of a commentary on the original *Dogmatics*, and here Bolt thought it appropriate to emphasize Bavinck's commitment to the centrality of his holistic creational doctrine.

17. Bavinck, *Essays on Religion, Science, and Society*, 250.

18. Bavinck, *Philosophy of Revelation*, 27, 64. Bavinck uses unity-in-diversity to uphold Christianity against evolutionism, monism, and Hegelianism.

19. Bavinck, *Reformed Dogmatics: God and Creation*, 438. Bavinck uses unity-in-diversity to correct paganism, pantheism, and materialism.

20. See the essays "Philosophy of Religion (Faith)" and "Of Beauty and Aesthetics" in Bavinck, *Essays on Religion, Science, and Society*, 30 and 259.

21. "While all creatures display vestiges of God, only a human being is the image of God" (Bavinck, *Reformed Dogmatics: God and Creation*, 555).

22. "Bavinck presents a unique assertion about the image of God, not seen in his predecessors: the body is an integral aspect of the image of God. In humanity's embodied creation as the image of God, . . . Bavinck understands the body as a crucial component of the image. Humans as individuals and humanity as a whole, unified while diverse, are the embodied image of God" (Joustra, "An Embodied *Imago Dei*," 17).

doctrine of the *imago Dei* quite literally fleshes out a doctrine of diversity. Any discussion of racial diversity must begin here. Indeed, "nothing in a human being is excluded from the image of God," including race.[23]

As with the rest of the creation, humanity was never meant to remain static. The *imago Dei* contained the promise of eschatological fulfillment, and so, from the beginning, creation was moving toward a yet-to-be-realized destination.[24] God intended humanity to expand from simple diversity into a vastly more pluriform diversity. Meditating on Genesis 2:24, Bavinck writes:

> From the beginning, it was the will of God that, as soon as more families arose, the man would leave his father and mother and would choose a wife as his helpmate . . . from another family. The wonderful expansion of the human race, the infinite variety among people, and the inexhaustible richness of relationships between households and families, generations and peoples, are all due to this divine will.[25]

Racial diversity was part of God's plan from the beginning, to populate a diverse creation with a diversifying humanity.

The entrance of sin does not alter this plan. When discussing the plurality of "distinctions and dissimilarities" in humanity and society, Bavinck states that "while all these things have undoubtedly been modified by sin and changed in appearance, they nevertheless have their . . . foundation in creation, in the ordinances of God, and not in sin."[26] Coupled with creational intent, divine providence guaranteed that "in all that division and brokenness, unity has been preserved."[27] Racial diversity, therefore, is not simply a product of sin. It remains grounded in God's plan for humanity. It is impossible to divorce human sin from the story of race, but it is still necessary to foster a Christian imagination that conceives of the *possibility* of a beautiful, racially diverse humanity, emanating from the garden of Eden as an outworking of God's creational plan.

This creation-positive protology became a hallmark of the Dutch Neo-Calvinist system. Theologians following Bavinck have elaborated upon the

23. Bavinck, *Reformed Dogmatics: God and Creation*, 555.

24. "At creation, humanity was still sub-eschatological; humanity was given. . . an eschatological vision to anticipate. This eschatological vision humanity anticipated already contained both the unity and the unfolded diversity of all humankind" (Joustra, "An Embodied *Imago Dei*," 13).

25. Bavinck, *Christian Family*, 16. While Bavinck does not specifically address race as the diversification of humanity based on the nexus of cultural and physical differences, his emphasis on "peoples" indicates a view of humanity that is broadly diverse.

26. Bavinck, *Reformed Dogmatics: God and Creation*, 576.

27. Bavinck, *Reformed Dogmatics: God and Creation*, 525.

theme of unity-in-diversity within creation. G. C. Berkouwer, one of the most prolific Neo-Calvinist theologians, states that Bavinck's insistence that God is the Creator of all things allows him to "honor the mystery of the individual personality . . . and do justice to the organic unity of the human race."[28] Al Wolters builds his ethics around the idea that creation is normative, specifically in the "unity and diversity of creational givens."[29] Finally, Gordon Spykman uses the creation narrative in Genesis to call for unity and diversity in practice: "the Genesis account discloses both the coherent unity and the rich diversity of the creation order. This pattern of diversified unity and unified diversity colors the entire story. . . . The life of the human community is also called to display unity in diversity and diversity in unity. Neither uniformity nor fragmentation is normative."[30] Diversity is part of God's character and something he loves, so he impressed diversity into creation and sustained it through providence. Creational diversity, and especially human diversity, reveals God's nature and character.

To the question, "Why diversity?" Bavinck holds up creation. The doctrine of creation teaches four things. First, diversity is rooted in the nature of God. Human diversity reflects God's glory, not merely cultural aesthetics. Second, diversity is part of God's purpose for creation. He designed creation to multiply in diversity, so racial diversity is simply part of maturing toward our eschatological destiny. We honor God's design as we work along the grain of his creational intentions.[31] Third, racial diversity is an active part of human unity. In an age characterized by racial tension, Bavinck's conviction that diversity unfolds unity in all its richness is a healing word. Finally, diversity is governed by providence. It is not simply a product of the fall, nor has it lost its purpose because of sin. This leads to the second component of a doctrine of diversity: eschatology.

---

28. Berkouwer, *Man*, 287. Berkouwer utilizes Bavinck here in the discussion of traducianism and the creation of the soul.

29. Wolters, *Creation Regained*, 10–11.

30. Spykman, *Reformational Theology*, 186–87. Spykman continues to show how this particular vision of the Christian worldview was developed by Kuyper and Bavinck and honed through further theologians, such as D. H. Vollenhoven and H. Dooyeverd, notable Neo-Calvinist philosophers; see Spykman, *Reformational Theology*, 189.

31. Bavinck, in *The Christian Family*, uses this principle to argue against incest, which would necessarily limit expanding human diversity. It can also be used to argue in favor of multiracial marriage and multiracial/cultural worship.

LAST THINGS: DIVERSITY IN BAVINCK'S DOCTRINE OF NEW CREATION

"And behold, a great multitude . . . from all tribes and peoples and languages . . ." (Rev 7:9)

The history of redemption showcases God redeeming diversity in his creation. For Bavinck, "the essence of Christian religion consists in the reality that the creation of the Father, ruined by sin, is restored in the death of the Son of God and re-created by the grace of the Holy Spirit into a kingdom of God."[32] Simply put, "grace restores nature."[33] Since nature includes diversity, redemption includes diversity, bringing his plans for human diversity to completion in Christ.

Bavinck's "grace restores nature" paradigm does not imply merely a return to unfallen creation. Rather, grace allows creation to move toward eschatological fulfillment: "in that way [the world] displays the attributes and perfections of God, in principle already at the outset, to an increasing degree as it develops, and perfectly at the end of the ages."[34] God's magnificent redemption in Christ is not simply "repristination" of the original creation, but one in which creation is "raised to a higher glory."[35] That is, God does not return creation to its immature glory, moments before Adam and Eve fell. God raises creation to the mature, eschatological glory he always intended, allowing his glory to shine in the completed creation: "grace restores nature and raises it to its highest pinnacle."[36] This approach helps magnify the abundance of grace present in Christ's redeeming work: "Christ gives more than sin stole."[37]

---

32. Bavinck, *Reformed Dogmatics: Prolegomena*, 112.

33. Wolters, *Creation Regained*, 12. This theme of grace restoring nature, which has become a hallmark of the Neo-Calvinist tradition, is explored in depth in Veenhof, *Nature and Grace in Herman Bavinck*. Veenhof argues that Bavinck's entire theological project is built on this redemptive relationship between nature and grace, in opposition to Catholic, Lutheran, Anabaptist, and other traditions.

34. Bavinck, *Reformed Dogmatics: God and Creation*, 436. This line of thinking is consistent with the broader Reformed conception of a covenant of works. Though this was and is an area of intramural debate, the essence involves the belief that Adam's tenure in the garden involved a probationary period with the expectation of creational growth and maturity as humanity, under Adam's headship, progressed toward the eschaton. For a discussion of the various views present in the Reformed community, see Letham, *Westminster Assembly*, 226–32.

35. See Veenhof, *Nature and Grace in Herman Bavinck*, 24–25.

36. Bavinck, *Reformed Dogmatics: Sin and Salvation in Christ*, 577.

37. Bavinck, "Common Grace," 59. My thanks to Dr. Jessica Joustra for pointing out this wonderful quote.

Bavinck's theology of redemption—grace restoring nature to its highest glory—has far-reaching consequences for a doctrine of racial diversity. In the new heaven and earth, creational diversity will be brought to maturity and purified, leading to a superabundance of redeemed diversity: "All that is true, honorable, just, pure, pleasing, and commendable in the whole of creation, in heaven and on earth, is gathered up in the future city of God—renewed, recreated, boosted to its highest glory."[38] Though there will be only one community—God's people—in the new creation:

> in that community, which Christ has purchased and gathered from all nations, languages, and tongues, all nations, Israel included, maintain their distinct place and calling. And all those nations—each in accordance with its own distinct national character—bring into the new Jerusalem all they have received from God in the way of glory and honor.[39]

In keeping with its Trinitarian imprint, God's new creation possesses profound diversity contained within an awe-inspiring unity. By extension, such redeemed diversity includes racial diversity.

This side of the new Jerusalem, racial difference often manifests itself in disunity, but when sin is purged, racial difference becomes a gift: "the great diversity that exists among people in all sorts of ways is not destroyed in eternity but is cleansed from all that is sinful and made serviceable to fellowship with God and each other."[40] All forms of human diversity will be cleansed of sin to promote the wonders of flourishing and happiness: "tribes, peoples, and nations all make their own particular contribution to the enrichment of life in the new Jerusalem."[41]

The theme of diversity is so integral to Bavinck's theology that it is found up to the final paragraph of his four-volume *Dogmatics*, in which he considers the place of eternal rewards. Here too, diversity is not static. In the eschaton, God not only protects diversity but ensures that it proliferates. Why, Bavinck asks, would God highlight differences, even going so far as to crown some with greater glory than others?:

> His purpose in doing this . . . is that, on earth as it is in heaven, there would be a profuse diversity in the believing community, and that in such diversity the glory of his attributes would be manifest. Indeed, as a result of this diversity, the life of fellowship

---

38. Bavinck, *Reformed Dogmatics: Holy Spirit, Church, and New Creation*, 720.
39. Bavinck, *Reformed Dogmatics: Holy Spirit, Church, and New Creation*, 720.
40. Bavinck, *Reformed Dogmatics: Holy Spirit, Church, and New Creation*, 727.
41. Bavinck, *Reformed Dogmatics: Holy Spirit, Church, and New Creation*, 727.

with God and with the angels, and of the blessed among themselves, gains in depth and intimacy. In that fellowship everyone has a place and task of one's own, based on personality and character . . . All creatures will then live and move and have their being in God, who is all in all, who reflects all his attributes in the mirror of his works and glorifies himself in them.[42]

This new creation will resound with the fullness of God, who has brought out all the innate fullness of creation in marvelous unity-in-diversity, for the delight of his creation and the glory of his name. The crowning achievement of this redeemed diversity is renewed humanity—diverse, embodied, racial humanity—existing together as one people of God.[43]

This eschatological vision of redeemed diversity is the logical and biblical conclusion to Bavinck's creation-positive protology. It forms the second necessary component of a doctrine of diversity: knowing the end of the story is just as important as knowing the beginning. As Anthony Hoekema, a biblical theologian from the Dutch tradition, writes, "the doctrine of the new earth is important for a proper grasp of the full dimensions of God's redemptive program . . . The total work of Christ is nothing less than to redeem this entire creation from the effects of sin."[44] Purified from the fragmentary forces of sin, racial and ethnic identity are ennobled by "the gospel of the coming kingdom which sweeps the redeemable aspects of human culture along into the 'new Jerusalem.'"[45] This vision of redeemed diversity offers yet another answer to the question, "Why diversity?" In the eschaton, rather than being a point of division, racial difference is purified to be a gift to others and a valuable component of humanity's worship of God. God is glorified precisely as his racially diverse people come together in redemptive unity and love.

THE CHURCH IN BETWEEN: DIVERSITY IN BAVINCK'S ECCLESIOLOGY

"Here there is not Greek and Jew, circumcised and uncircumcised, barbarian, Scythian, slave, free; but Christ is all, and in all." (Col 3:11)

---

42. Bavinck, *Reformed Dogmatics: Holy Spirit, Church, and New Creation*, 729–30.

43. Bavinck, *Reformed Dogmatics: Holy Spirit, Church, and New Creation*, 729.

44. Hoekema, *Bible and the Future*, 274–75. This is the broad consensus of the Reformed community, as indicated by both Berkof and Berkouwer (Berkhof, *Systematic Theology*, 737; Berkouwer, *Return of Christ*, 221).

45. Spykman, *Reformational Theology*, 558.

After soaring in the heights of this glorious future, how can we not lament when we see the fragmentation of modern life? The existence of such profound racial disunity ought to break our hearts, when compared to the absolute bliss of redeemed life, in which racial diversity plays a crucial part. Redeemed diversity is beautiful: racial strife will be put to rest, and racial distinction will be a glorious gift that promotes Christian worship and human fellowship. Redeemed diversity is also motivating: these longings are meant to shape our life in the present. Having anchored the doctrine of diversity in first and last things, Bavinck weaves a robust theology of diversity for the "already/not yet" people of God, the church in between.

Two key aspects of Bavinck's ecclesiology have bearing on the discussion of racial diversity. First, there is an indicative truth: the present and the future are eschatologically connected. The future is brought, in part, into the present as an "already/not yet" reality. Second, there is an ethical imperative: because the future is only partially present, there is a remaining gap between experience and expectation that calls for action. God's people have an ethical mandate to continue working to realize God's redemptive vision in the present.

First, the indicative: in Christ, God's future kingdom is brought partially to bear in the present. "The kingdom is not entirely 'other worldly' but has been established by Christ upon earth . . . nevertheless, it is just as true that the kingdom is not exhaustively present in this life, it is not merely 'this worldly.' The kingdom *is* and *becomes*."[46] This "already/not yet" character of the kingdom means that the blessings of salvation, which are distinctly future-oriented, are partially enjoyed by believers in the present: "All the benefits that Christ has acquired for his own are not just bestowed in the state of glory but are in principle already granted here on earth . . . even participation in the divine nature is not something for the future alone but a goal envisaged already by the granting of God's promises here on earth."[47] This eschatological connection establishes a deep communion between God and his people. Here on earth, believers possess fellowship with God and, mysteriously, with the heavenly church and eschatological communion of

---

46. Bavinck, "Kingdom of God," 152 (emphasis original).

47. Bavinck, *Reformed Dogmatics: God and Creation*, 542–43. Bavinck cites 1 Corinthians 2:9, 2 Peter 1:4, and Hebrews 12:10 as supporting passages. When discussing the present reality and future promise of the kingdom, Bavinck consistently characterizes the present as possessing the future blessings of God "in principle" now, while hoping for the fullness of the promise in the future.

saints.[48] Though this fellowship will be perfected in the eschaton, "in principle it already exists on earth."[49]

The eschatological blessings of salvation include diversity: Bavinck states that "the kingdom of God is the highest, the most perfect community ... There the richest harmony rules with the perfection of beauty. There the most glorious and purest unity reigns among the most inscrutable wealth and the most incalculable diversity."[50] The church's diversity points to the redeeming work of Christ, who created "in himself one new man" (Eph 2:15) out of enemy peoples. Indeed, as Spykman writes, "the redeeming work of Christ in and through the church does not wipe out [diversities in ethnic origin, locality, language, and culture], but sanctifies them by incorporating them into a more encompassing unity."[51] The racial differences embedded into humanity as an expression of the *imago Dei* and secured as part of the glory of the new creation are sanctified to form a tangible portion of the church's present identity. As the multiracial kingdom takes root in the here-and-now, the redeemed diversity of the eschaton, marked by beauty and abundance, becomes part of the church's kaleidoscopic visage in the present-tense.

This is true even with the coexisting reality of racial division. Reflecting on the presence of church division, Bavinck writes:

> Undoubtedly, the divisions of the church of Christ are caused by sin; in heaven, there will no longer be any room for them. But this is far from being the whole story. In unity God loves the diversity. Among all creatures there was diversity even when as yet there was no sin. As a result of sin that diversity has been perverted and corrupted, but diversity as such is good and important also for the church ... [Christ] takes all [of the] differences into his service and adorns his church with them. Indeed, though the division of humanity into peoples and languages was occasioned by sin, it has something good in it, which is brought into the church and thus preserved for all eternity. From many races and languages and peoples and nations Christ gathered his church on earth.[52]

---

48. Bavinck, *Reformed Dogmatics: Holy Spirit, Church, and New Creation*, 723.

49. Bavinck, *Reformed Dogmatics: Holy Spirit, Church, and New Creation*, 723.

50. Bavinck, "Kingdom of God," 144–45. Note again the theme of abundance in Bavinck's thought.

51. Spykman, *Reformational Theology*, 444.

52. Bavinck, *Reformed Dogmatics: Holy Spirit, Church, and New Creation*, 318.

In this quotation, we see a compact treatment of the reality of race from a theological perspective. The good of race is present, in seed form, as part of human creation. Though the actual pluriformity of humanity's racial diversity came about through sin, it was always intended to move in that direction. The world stumbles over racial diversity, allowing it to become divisive. But in the church, racial difference is purified of its divisiveness to become a true unity-in-diversity. It must be so; in spite of its imperfect state, the kingdom on earth still reflects God's own unity-in-diversity.

In the church's racial diversity in the present, we see the gradual fulfillment of God's plan to fill his creation with abundant diversity. The diversity of the church on earth is not an accidental happenstance, but a glorious sign of our salvation. However, because of the presence of sin, our diversity often manifests itself in fragmentation, not praise-filled pluriformity.[53] Thus, the church possesses her glorious diversity as a diamond in the rough, with the call to bring forth the riches of racial diversity through redemptive action.

This call to pursue redeemed diversity forms the second aspect of Bavinck's ecclesiology: the ethical imperative. As the kingdom takes root in the here-and-now, and as Christians imagine the redeemed diversity of the eschatological kingdom with its beauty and abundance, securing that destiny becomes part of our mission. Seeing our destiny invites us to pursue its realization in the now.

This ethical mandate is seen most clearly as Bavinck addresses two attributes of the church: unity and catholicity. In the *Reformed Dogmatics*, Bavinck addresses the attributes of the church ("one, holy, catholic, and apostolic") to distinguish the Reformed tradition from the Roman Catholic Church. To Bavinck, the Roman Catholic overinstitutionalizes the church's attributes. According to Rome, the church is united in the institution, and it is catholic because it is a global institution.[54] Against this, Bavinck insists that the church is first and foremost a community, an organism, not primarily an institution. Therefore, the attributes are essentially spiritual, not institutional. The unity of the church comes from worshiping the same Lord through the same Holy Spirit, celebrating the same baptism, and holding to

---

53. Berkouwer, reflecting on the conversation about unity versus uniformity, states, "We sense a certain richness in the doctrine of pluriformity. . .[which] makes room for variegation and distinction, both of which are so valuable for all human life: because reality is not captive to uniformity, it is richer, not poorer!" Channeling Bavinck, Berkouwer demonstrates that unity-in-diversity leads to abundance (See Berkouwer, *Church*, 52).

54. Bavinck, *Reformed Dogmatics: Holy Spirit, Church, and New Creation*, 320–24.

the same faith. The catholicity of the church stems from the universality of the faith and the call to preach the gospel to the nations across the globe.[55]

However, though the attributes are primarily spiritual, they require an outward manifestation. Christians cannot content themselves with holding the attributes spiritually, while denying them in their lifestyle. Bavinck will not allow Reformed Christians to cling to the idea of the invisible church to the detriment of the visible.[56] Christ did not come to institute an invisible church, but a visible one; after all, the visible church is simply "the perspective of [the church's] witness and life."[57] Since the attributes of the church contain an ethical bite, the church cannot merely possess unity and catholicity spiritually and inwardly. It must pursue unity and catholicity in concrete church life.[58]

The church's unity and catholicity call Christians to a living and active embrace of unity-in-diversity. The unity of the church "is in the process of becoming" and is seen "in that which all Christian churches have in common," including articles of common faith, such as the Apostles' Creed.[59] Unity is hindered by any undue separation of churches, and "Christians cannot humble [themselves] deeply enough over the schisms and discord that have existed all through the centuries in the church of Christ. It is a sin against God."[60] In a world broken by sin and in a culture beset by racial fragmentation, the unity of the church must be preserved. Race and ethnicity cannot divide the church, for Christ relativizes all our differences: "that which unites all true Christians is always more than that which separates them."[61]

---

55. Bavinck, *Reformed Dogmatics: Holy Spirit, Church, and New Creation*, 321–23.

56. Berkouwer laments that some in the Reformed camp abused "the concept of the invisible church. . . not so much to expose the tensions and responsibilities of the visible church as to 'solve' those tensions, especially with respect to unity." Thus, for Berkouwer, as well as Bavinck, the church's invisible identity is meant to act as her conscience, not as her bomb shelter (Berkouwer, *Church*, 38).

57. Bavinck, *Reformed Dogmatics: Holy Spirit, Church, and New Creation*, 306.

58. In *Our Reasonable Faith*, Bavinck describes overcoming cultural barriers as one of the primary goals of Paul's ministry in Acts and in his letters, and thus unity also belongs to the church as a goal (Bavinck, *Our Reasonable Faith*, 523; see also Spykman, *Reformational Theology*, 443).

59. Bavinck, *Our Reasonable Faith*, 523; Bavinck, *Reformed Dogmatics: Holy Spirit, Church, and New Creation*, 321. Bavinck refers to the creed, the "Twelve Articles of Faith," as something that unites all Christians.

60. Bavinck, *Reformed Dogmatics: Holy Spirit, Church, and New Creation*, 316.

61. Bavinck, *Reformed Dogmatics: Holy Spirit, Church, and New Creation*, 321. Berkouwer similarly states that, "in light of [the teaching of Acts 10 that God does not discriminate], whatever differences, there is no 'distinction' in Christ" (Berkouwer, *Church*, 125).

However, unity must be won by embracing diversity, not by papering over it. The catholicity of the church leaves no room for "color-blind Christianity." Bavinck insists "Christianity is a world religion suited and intended for every people and age, for every class and rank, for every time and place."[62] Therefore, "that church is most catholic that most clearly expresses in its confession and applies in its practice this international and cosmopolitan character of the Christian religion."[63] Seen in this light, catholicity is the only acceptable posture of a church shaped by a gospel that applies to the whole person and the whole of humanity. As such, catholicity necessarily includes race: "The gospel is a joyful tiding, not only for the individual person but also for humanity, for the family, for society, for the state, for art and science, for the entire cosmos, for the whole groaning creation."[64] In its social and theological catholicity, the church embodies the gospel. This gospel promises nothing less than the redemption of embodied, racial humanity, made in the image of God, reflecting his unity-in-diversity. As the church demonstrates its catholicity in action, "the richness, the many-sidedness, the pluriformity of the Christian faith" is proclaimed.[65]

The church's catholicity stands as an indictment of Christians who refuse to pursue diversity. For, as Berkouwer states, "it becomes clear that the whole life of the church—both doctrine and practice—is related to the critical testing of catholicity, for every violation of the mystery of the truth of salvation—in word and deed, in confessional, political, or social heresy—can obscure the outlook on the qualitative richness of the whole." Christians well-versed in confessional and political heresies must also consider which "social heresies" corrupt the church's catholicity, including the sin of racism.[66]

These social heresies destroy catholicity, because "catholicity implies the mutuality of Christian fellowship everywhere, reciprocal relations, and solidarity with all who belong to the household of faith in their cross-bearing as well as their crowning achievements."[67] Catholicity demands *orthopraxy* as much as *orthodoxy*. It demands practical racial inclusion, not merely doctrinal agreement with the early church's ecumenical counsels. It rejects any hint of partiality or prejudice, it is repulsed by any whiff of

---

62. Bavinck, *Reformed Dogmatics: Holy Spirit, Church, and New Creation*, 323.
63. Bavinck, *Reformed Dogmatics: Holy Spirit, Church, and New Creation*, 323.
64. Bavinck, "Catholicity of Christianity," 224.
65. Bavinck, "Catholicity of Christianity," 250.
66. Berkouwer, *Church*, 121. Berkouwer's treatment of catholicity is a profoundly beautiful exposition of the ethical implications of the church's confession.
67. Spykman, *Reformational Theology*, 447.

sectarianism. Racism, sexism, and ethnocentrism have no part in God's holy *catholic* church.[68] Because the church is united and catholic, Christians must embrace an ethic of racial inclusion.

For those who wonder if Bavinck's theological mind outgrew the Reformed tradition on this point, his teaching on unity and catholicity is nothing more than a working out of the Westminster Standards. The Westminster Confession of Faith teaches that the communion of saints requires active unity in diversity: "being united to one another in love, they have communion in each other's gifts and graces, and are obliged to the performance of such duties, public and private, as do conduce to their mutual good, both in the inward and outward man."[69] And these obligations are due, not merely to those Christians with shared affinities, but to all Christians: "[this] communion, as God offers opportunity, is to be extended unto all those who, in every place, call upon the name of the Lord Jesus."[70] The Westminster writers viewed the scriptural mandate of love within the church to be holistic and inclusive, pushing diverse believers toward each other, to flourish in relationship: "ultimately this love for each other cannot be restricted to what we have; it needs to encompass who we are."[71]

"Why diversity?" Because God loves the whole world—his entire multiracial creation—and Christians must as well.[72] Diversity is part of the church's DNA, her interrelated attributes. To be truly catholic is to be truly united in diversity, and true unity requires the diversity protected by catholicity. As Christians of different races come together in the church, we show forth our unity and catholicity to the glory of God.

TOWARD A REDEMPTIVE DOCTRINE OF DIVERSITY

Through an examination of Herman Bavinck's theology, the church gains a doctrine of diversity composed of three essential pieces: a creation-positive protology, a diversity-redeeming eschatology, and an ecclesiology marked by unified catholicity. In these, the silver thread is unity-in-diversity, rooted in God's character, mirrored in God's creation, secured by God's salvation, all for the sake of God's glory. To a denomination "true to the Reformed

68. Clowney, *Church*, 97.
69. *Westminster Confession of Faith*, 26.1.
70. *Westminster Confession of Faith*, 26.2.
71. Van Dixhoorn, *Confessing the Faith*, 352. My thanks to Dr. Irwyn Ince for this reference.
72. See Bavinck, "Catholicity of Christianity," 246–47.

faith," these Reformed tenets contribute to a praxis of racial inclusivity. While Bavinck is correct to offer some words of patience—only Christ can accomplish the perfection of unity and diversity and will only accomplish it at his second coming—his theology of diversity is robust enough to hold the weight of Christ's call to be one body, including, respecting, and embracing racial differences.[73]

Can there be outsiders inside God's people, excluded because of race or culture? No, because racism sins against Christ's unified, catholic church. Should we pursue redeemed diversity in our congregations and denomination, even at great expense of resources? Yes, because this redeemed diversity, with insiders of all races and cultures, forms our witness to redemption in Christ for a watching world. Why diversity? Ultimately, because it glorifies our gloriously diverse God. Thus, to be "true to the Reformed faith," the PCA must prize, protect, and pursue true racial diversity. Far from being captive to a fleeting cultural preference, pursuing racial diversity is one of the most Reformed things a PCA church can do.

---

73. Bavinck, "Catholicity of Christianity," 250–51; Bavinck, "Kingdom of God," 169–70.

PART II

Racial Hospitality in the PCA

4

Charting the Minority Experience

Toward a Phenomenology of Black PCA Pastors

THE PCA WAS FORMED in 1973 to be "Faithful to the Scriptures, True to the Reformed faith, Obedient to the great commission of Jesus Christ," with aspirations of welcoming people of all races. The two questions guiding this study have been 1) How does a theology of racial inclusion intersect with the theological commitments of the PCA motto; and 2) How is the PCA living up to its aim of racial inclusion? Chapters 2 and 3 answered the first question: the Bible and the Reformed tradition should empower our approach to race and reconciliation. As Chapter 2 explored, the narrative sweep of the Scriptures, of which the Great Commission is an important part, is toward greater inclusion of races within the church. Within the citizenship of God's city, there are to be no outsiders separated by false boundaries. As Chapter 3 argued, the Reformed tradition builds upon this foundation, adding a doctrinal emphasis on diversity within the church. To answer the first question, for the PCA to fully live up to its motto it must actively pursue racial reconciliation. We now need to explore the second question: How is the PCA living up to its aim of racial inclusion?

RESEARCH METHODOLOGY: LISTENING TO HUMAN EXPERIENCES

There are two approaches for answering this question: quantitative and qualitative analyses. A quantitative approach would collect and analyze numerical data related to ethnicity with the goal of producing a statistical picture of the denomination. For instance, a quantitative study could measure diversity by calculating the percentages of minority members. A denomination whose demographics match or exceed the diversity of its surrounding population could be declared a racially inclusive organization.[1] However, quantitative analysis has its shortcomings. It fails to give a robust picture of human relationships and does not automatically account for the perception of welcome—just because one is a member does not mean one feels included. Similarly, while a statistical model can offer big-picture demographics, it needs interpretation. Are the percentages good or bad? At what point have we achieved diversity? Who gets to decide the goal in the first place? Demographic studies can also lead to triumphalism if the numbers are good, or fatalistic pessimism if the numbers are bad, or to insensitive tokenism if minorities are recruited simply to boost statistics. For these reasons, a quantitative analysis needs another resource to offer necessary nuance.

Such is the purpose of qualitative studies. A qualitative approach offers a thick description of racial inclusion, helping readers inhabit the lived experience of minorities by listening to their testimonies and add further nuance to the analytical question.[2] Qualitative analysis, then, is a conver-

---

1. Interestingly, a 2015 Pew Research study (Lipka, "Most and Least Racially Diverse U.S. Religious Groups") showed that the PCA was more racially diverse than most Protestant denominations. This study is instructive for two reasons: first, the PCA does indeed need to grow in racial diversity. Even though it ranked higher in diversity than many denominations, it received a 4.4 index score, with a denominational make-up of 80 percent White, 6 percent Black, 3 percent Asian, 5 percent Other, and 6 percent Latino, as compared to the US adult population of 66 percent White, 12 percent Black, 4 percent Asian, 4 percent Other, and 15 percent Latino (the US receives a 6.6 index score for diversity). Second, the PCA ranked higher in diversity than many of the theologically progressive denominations that have a greater external emphasis on diversity. For example, at the time of this writing, the United Church of Christ (UCC) website leads with this phrase: "We are a distinct and diverse community of Christians that come together as one church united in Spirit to love all, welcome all and seek justice for all," whereas the PCA website simply hosts its motto: "Faithful to the Scriptures, True to the Reformed Faith, and Obedient to the Great Commission." Yet according to the Pew study, the UCC scored a 2.5 on the diversity index, compared to the PCA's 4.4. A similar finding occurs when comparing the websites of the Evangelical Lutheran Church, the Presbyterian Church (USA), and the Episcopal Church, with their diversity index scores (1.0, 2.8, and 2.3 respectively). These churches outwardly laud diversity more than the PCA, but struggle to achieve diversity in their congregations. This suggests that the PCA's stance on Scripture and theology may actually contribute to racial diversity, rather than detract from it, a suggestion that will be borne out over many of the following interviews with Black PCA pastors. If this is the case, a remaining question must be asked: If the PCA's doctrine contributes to diversity, what about the PCA's culture hinders it?

2. Hence the research question "*How* is the PCA living up to its aim?," rather than simply "*Is* the PCA living up to its aim?"

sational exploration where the testimonies of individuals weave together a collective, experiential narrative, or phenomenology.

John Creswell defines the goal of phenomenology as "the essence of a lived phenomenon," with the goal of "understanding the essence of the experience."[3] Phenomenology utilizes interviews and other observational methods to grasp this essence and describe the lived experiences of others.[4] Theologically, this approach has many strengths. It appreciates the significance of community and relationships for meaning, and upholds peoples' dignity by assuming that their experiences offer legitimate insights into the truth. As an analytical method, phenomenology grants legitimacy to lived experience without necessarily granting it supremacy over other forms of knowledge; it can be used with humility to gain insight, as one of many resources.

The Christian tradition supports much of this. As embodied persons, humans were created to exist within community (Gen 2:18), and human relationships form a critical part of understanding and interpreting history (Deut 6:20–25). Made in God's image, human persons possess dignity, reason, and observational sense, which God uses as vessels of his revelation (Gen 1:26; Prov 6:6–11; Ps 19:1). As such, Christians can appreciate both objective observations and subjective experiences as complementary components of God's truth. The doctrine of sin grants that phenomenology is incomplete. Lived experience is never infallible, and in the context of a loving and trusting community, experiences can be scrutinized and interpretations disputed. However, the doctrine of sin also pushes Christians to admit that prejudice causes people to dismiss the experiences of others (Exod 23:6; Deut 16:19–20), so phenomenology helpfully prizes the insights of those often ignored, ensuring they have a seat at the table. Phenomenology is a useful—even pastoral—tool for Christian inquiry. The following chapters present a phenomenology of Black PCA pastors, offering the essence of their lived experience within the denomination.

To construct this phenomenology, I interviewed twelve Black pastors in the PCA.[5] These pastors were church planters, associate pastors, de-

---

3. Creswell and Poth, *Qualitative Inquiry and Research Design*, 104.

4. Creswell and Poth, *Qualitative Inquiry and Research Design*, 104–5.

5. I generated my sample through two methods: convenience sampling and snowball sampling. "Convenience sampling means recruiting whomever you have access to. Snowball sampling means starting with a convenience sample of a few research participants and asking them to select others" (Auerbach and Silverstein, *Qualitative Data*, 18). In keeping with the qualitative method, I conducted interviews until I reached "theoretical saturation"; i.e., the interview stage concluded once the interviews stopped providing new or contrasting evidence. These methods generated an interview panel of twelve pastors, varying in both age and career tenure, ranging from six to twenty-five years of ordained ministry. Because these men are more easily identifiable due to the

nominational leaders, and pastors of long-established churches. They have ministered in urban, inner-city, and suburban churches, with a variety of congregational demographics: predominantly White, predominantly Black, and racially blended.

The interviews were constructed around five questions:

1. As an African American, what was it like for you to come into the PCA?
2. What is your experience of ministry in the PCA?
3. Why are you committed to the PCA?
4. How can the PCA be supportive of you as an African American minister?
5. Who or what ministries are currently very supportive of you and your ministry?

These five research questions provided the main structure for the interviews, but the tone of the interview was conversational. I would frequently ask other related questions to help me understand their experiences more fully. The goal of these questions was developing a thick narrative aimed at answering the larger phenomenological question, "What does it feel like to be Black in the PCA?"

A few struggled with the label "African American," either because they were born outside of the USA or because they had biracial parents. I felt that their stories needed to be included, because as one pastor put it, "I've spent most of my adult life in America as a Black man . . . Nobody ever stops me on the street and says 'Hey, before I discriminate against you, are you a Black man born in America or are you from [another country]?'"[6] Their stories add an additional layer of nuance to the question of identity and belonging.

With the goal of presenting the essence of a lived experience, the interview content needed to be structured into a framework, distilling various testimonies into the shared essence.[7] The initial interviews generated a list of repeating ideas.[8] These repeating ideas were then organized into broader themes. The broader themes were finally distilled into three abstract theoretical constructs and named. For some, the names came directly from the interviewees; for others, I offered a name that seemed to capture the essence

---

small numbers of PCA Black pastors, I have used pseudonyms to protect their confidentiality. I have also obscured certain personal details to protect their identity.

6. Another pastor expressed the challenge of finding identity within the Black/African American paradigm: "It's a difficult thing for most Africans living in America to find their identity because you almost feel like you don't belong anywhere. As much as you tried to identify with one group, you cannot. You do not belong."

7. Creswell and Poth, *Qualitative Inquiry and Research Design*, 105.

8. See Auerbach and Silverstein, *Qualitative Data*, 31–76.

of that experience most accurately. From these theoretical constructs, a phenomenological narrative emerges.[9]

For this narrative to reflect the voices of the interviewees, I used their own words, whenever possible. For shorter quotations and simpler concepts, I attempted to weave the quotes into a seamless narrative. When the conversational back-and-forth yielded powerful comments, I included my question in bold in the traditional style for written interviews. Finally, when their stories seemed too important to redact or summarize, or when the majority of the interviewees testified to a similar experience, I simply included the entire excerpt from the interview transcripts, in order to convey, if possible, the weight of their collective experience.

THE ESSENCE OF LIVED EXPERIENCE

So, what does it feel like to be Black in the PCA? It feels like being a sojourner, a person never fully home. The journey of being Black in the PCA has three distinct stages. The first stage is, almost universally, one of welcome and inclusion. But there comes a turning point, where the initial welcome wears off, leaving a growing sense of remaining an outsider. This stage is often marked by fatigue and frustration. At this point, each pastor faces a decision to stay or leave. At this crossroads of welcome and fatigue, these pastors chose the path of resilience, learning to thrive within the culture. These three theoretical constructs or movements demonstrate the joys and frustrations of ministering as an ultra-minority within a primarily White denomination.

Table 1: The Experience of Black Pastors

A Journey in Three Stages

Stage 1: Being Welcomed into the Denomination
1. Sharing theology
2. Appreciating the ministry
3. Receiving hospitality

Stage 2: Experiencing Racial Fatigue as an Outsider
1. Experiencing numerical isolation
2. Experiencing loss
3. Experiencing cultural conflict and theological isolation

Stage 3: Learning to Thrive
1. Committing to the PCA
2. Embracing a shared biblical-theological tradition
3. Forming life-giving relationships
4. Thinking strategically about the future
5. Practicing gratitude

---

9. See Table 1.

5

Welcome to the PCA!

NONE OF THE BLACK TEs interviewed began life as an evangelical Presbyterian in the PCA. They all came to the denomination through one road or another, and largely received a hearty initial welcome. This welcome involves shared theological convictions, meaningful church interactions, and personal hospitality.

> Table 2: Being Welcomed into the Denomination
> Stage One of the Journey
>
> 1. Sharing theology
> 2. Appreciating the ministry
> 3. Receiving hospitality

SHARING THEOLOGY

Of the twelve pastors interviewed, eleven explicitly stated during the interview that Reformed theology was the reason that they came to or stayed in the PCA. While one pastor grew up in a Reformed denomination overseas, for many, the transition into the PCA began with a new conviction for Reformed theology and then searching for a Reformed church. Shelton described Reformed theology as "an epiphany—'Wow, this really helps me understand the Scriptures.'" For Desmond, the process was similar: "I embraced Reformed theology. It wasn't something I was studying at the time. It was studying through Scripture where I embraced it. I didn't know anyone who was Reformed." Terrance began his journey to Reformed theology in seminary. Through studying the texts, "it just became more and more clear I'm really Reformed." For Brian, finding a Reformed church was a simple conclusion: "I fell in love with the doctrine."

Some pastors found that Reformed theology fit well with their cultural experience, that their experience as Black men gave them an intuitive appreciation for the system. As Martin said when studying the Westminster Standards in church, "That's stuff I believed already. It was just spelled out better, more clearly and that kind of thing. But it's stuff we're already familiar with. I mean, like being African American—the sovereignty of God . . . of course you believe in that, from your life experience. You know the doctrines of providence and things like that. It makes perfect sense."

The PCA is known for its commitment to orthodoxy, which attracted many of these pastors. Even before joining the PCA, Alexander admitted that "the doctrines and the principles upon which the PCA was founded, I found to be very compelling. I've found [the PCA] to be a denomination that's willing to hold the line at a time when holding the line is counterintuitive. And we do it in such a way as to, I think, be winsome." As André summarized, "I'm just glad to be in a denomination that's committed to orthodoxy . . . I think we have a robust denomination that's really committed to God's word."

The organization and the polity of the church was also appealing to a few pastors. Alexander noted that, coming from a Baptist background, he was drawn to the PCA in part because of its polity. Anthony also noted the appeal of the polity: "It's not a matter of salvation to me, but in terms of the functioning and the running of the church, I really appreciate the system."

This sense of a shared theology continues to play a role in Black pastors staying in the denomination. When asked why he stayed in the PCA, Brian immediately answered, "Theology. I believe it's biblical . . . I trust it. I trust the system. I trust Calvinism." As Terrance expressed, "There's no other place I feel that would be good for me. It is still a place where I think there's a good fit confessionally and I think the conversations that are happening within our camp of the Reformed Presbyterian world are heading in the right direction."

APPRECIATING THE MINISTRY

In addition to sharing the theology of the church, these Black pastors appreciated elements of their experience at the local church. For those that were newer to the PCA, the denomination itself was irrelevant; the ministry was essential. For Martin, "I came to a church that I was drawn to, that preached the gospel, that was in the inner city, that was doing works of justice and mercy, preaching the Scriptures, and it was multiethnic and really wanting to be involved in that. And it happened to be PCA; I didn't know what the PCA was until I was there. And so I was drawn to the church and the pastor there." Anthony, who joined the PCA during seminary with a calling toward inner-city ministry, stated, "That was my first experience in terms of actually working in a PCA church . . . I was drawn to that type of ministry. It wasn't so much me going to the PCA because of its governance or its history or things like that. It's in many ways my first work experience in that particular context, and it so happened to be PCA."

For some, the individual churches themselves modeled a winsome form of diversity, which acted as a cushion between them and the larger racial dynamics in the denomination. Shelton appreciated seeing Black leadership at his church and enjoyed a diverse worship experience. Thomas enjoyed the mix of people at his urban church, with a variety of social stages and ethnicities present, and the intellectual, eclectic worship led by talented individuals. The impact of the sermon was especially important. While Jimmy was unfamiliar with the PCA at first, "I knew that I really appreciated what this guy was preaching and it really ministered to me." Fernando had a similar sentiment: "I enjoyed the preaching; it spoke to me intellectually." Thomas's first encounters with the PCA were in an urban environment, and the emphasis on contextualization was particularly appealing: "It felt natural and inviting; it spoke to me. It reinvigorated Christianity for me. There were some other issues tied around that but it was mainly the fact that it spoke to me culturally."

RECEIVING HOSPITALITY

Personal hospitality was one of the ways these Black TEs felt most welcomed in the denomination. While noting some alienation within the broader church culture, these pastors received a warm and personal welcome. The extension of hospitality overcame some of the culture shock; although as the narrative bears out, hospitality did not always mean unconditional acceptance.

Many of these pastors expressed appreciation for the normal hospitality extended to them by the church congregations. Brian recounted his experience of receiving hospitality: "It was a very different worship experience, but I was always embraced. They just embraced and loved on us. How can you reject that?" Fernando experienced a similar expression of hospitality, highlighting the theme of welcome in his story: "I did not care for the music but the people welcomed me and that was important." At another church later in his journey, Fernando was also blessed by the hospitality of fellow church members: "They didn't culturally understand me. But they all welcomed me into their homes; they invited me over to dinner and they welcomed me into their lives." Alexander received similar welcome at the church where he was a member during seminary: "[the pastor] introduced me to several of the people there who loved me. They were gracious people." Terrance was excited to describe the hospitality of his second PCA church home: "Different types were in there and it was awesome. We just had an environment that was welcoming to everybody. It was awesome."

The hospitality of the pastor or an older mentor proved valuable to many of these pastors. Fernando described the hospitality of his first pastor as essential to his membership in the PCA: "He walked with me. He loved me. He welcomed me into his home . . . He was probably one of the biggest reasons why I'm in the denomination." A formative experience for Jimmy's journey was when a prominent PCA minister took a personal interest in him and his family: "We didn't know who they were, but they loved us, they took interest in us, they invited us over . . . [this was] hospitality." For Alexander, personal mentorship and hospitality led him to ministry in the PCA: "[An older (White) man] became my father in every respect. He loved me and cared for me. He never once treated me like I was a special case. It was very organic . . . He said, 'Listen I believe that you should be a member of the PCA.' He said, 'I know there are not a lot of Black men in the PCA and I don't know what that's going to mean for your career.' But he said, 'I believe God is calling you into the ministry.'"

Some pastors find the local presbytery to be a place of hospitality as well. Terrance described his presbytery as a safe place, exhibiting "openness to people of all ethnicities, walks of life. They were welcoming." Alexander's first experience with the presbytery was similarly positive: "I was warmly received. There was never pushback. I was encouraged to be on committees. I have never felt like I was excluded or included just because of my race. I always felt like I got the same fair shake as everybody else in the denomination."

6

Outsiders on the Inside

"Our experience was one of always feeling like outsiders."[1] Though these pastors were initially welcomed inside the denomination, eventually the realization dawned that they were still outsiders. Cultural barriers remained in place, and these minority pastors routinely experienced a sense of isolation within the larger denomination. There is a notable spectrum of the pastors' overall ministry experience in the PCA, from great pain to much rejoicing with relatively little trauma; however, each pastor articulated the strain of being an outsider in the denomination because of his race. This strain came from numerical isolation, a sense of loss, conflict, and theological isolation.

---

1. Interview with Brian.

> **Table 3: Experiencing Racial Fatigue as an Outsider**
>
> Stage Two of the Journey
>
> 1. Experiencing numerical isolation
> 2. Experiencing loss
>   * Sense of betrayal
>   * Loss of comfort and sense of home
>   * Loss of connection with the Black Church
> 3. Experiencing cultural conflict and theological isolation
>   * Cultures in conflict
>   * Racial isolation: Experience and articulation of racial dynamics
>   * Worldview isolation: Interpretation of history, dynamics of oppression, and cultural events
>   * Experiencing paternalism, marginalization, and microaggressions
>   * Pressure to conform
>   * Restricted sense of identity: "I can't be my full self."

EXPERIENCING NUMERICAL ISOLATION

Almost every Black pastor interviewed clearly remembered the time they first noticed they were the only person of color in the room. Whether at the local church or at a denominational meeting, the extremely low numbers of other Black pastors soon became apparent. Brian's realization came about slowly during his time as a member of a PCA church, before attending seminary: "I was so used to living in a White world because I worked in a White world and I was so used to Corporate America being White, so it was kind of continuing my world that I had before. But eventually I began to notice that it was all White." Similarly, Fernando experienced the isolation of being the Black member of an all-White Church: "I was the only Black guy in this group. I was the only Black guy at the church." For Shelton, it was during the meeting with the Credentials Committee[2]: "When I met with the credentials committee, I didn't have a problem with the meeting or the questions. I didn't feel uncomfortable. I just noticed, 'Oh, I'm Black and all these guys are White.'" For André, it was the local Presbytery: "I was the only Black person in my Presbytery." Martin's first larger denominational experiences came with a sense of shock: "I didn't know that it was unique being an African American in the PCA until I think the first Presbytery meeting I went to. And it was me and [two others] were the only Black people in that

---

2. In the PCA, each presbytery has a committee of elders responsible for examining and approving candidates for ordination.

room of, I don't know, 100 people. And then my first General Assembly was a similar experience to that. So, I was like, 'Whoa where am I?'" Anthony's experience of isolation came about because of his ministry in impoverished inner cities: "On some level, I feel like I've been on an island because of the type of ministry I'm engaged in."

Such small numbers led to strange experiences of racial tokenism, such as being recruited for ministry simply on the basis of skin color. Brian recalls being approached at a General Assembly meeting and being offered an opportunity to plant a church. As Brian remembers, the pastor did not know him personally, "but I was Black. I was the only one there at the General Assembly! He was recruiting me, and he didn't even know me . . . This is a positive experience from one perspective, but on the other side it is kind of a negative experience in that, well you are the only Black person, and he doesn't know you, but he is ready to recruit you." As he sums it up, his experience of ministry in the PCA was "Very mixed. My first experience in ministry in the PCA was very mixed. Racially it was hard, because I was a 'onesie' in this environment."[3]

EXPERIENCING LOSS

Sense of Betrayal

For some pastors, the dawning sense of isolation came with a sense of betrayal. After an initial sense of welcome in the denomination, uncovering the racial baggage in Reformed history sent them reeling. Jimmy's experience is paradigmatic: "When I learned about all this stuff in the PCA, I felt betrayed all the more because I had already stopped building and connecting and networking [within the Black Church], so I would have to start all over again. So, I was stuck. Do I keep going forward with these people? Because now this seems very uncertain for my future. This does not bode well for me being able to minister to the people that I want to minister to." Martin expressed a similar sense of shock in my conversation with him:

> I didn't know the history or the context and things like that, at that point. That came later.
>
> WB: What was that like?
>
> You're like, 'Whoa where am I? What am I doing here?'

---

3. Numerous pastors used this language when describing their experience.

For others, the sense of betrayal came when relationships were tried because of cultural differences. When under fire or in conflict, allies and friends were hard to find. In Martin's words, "I would have loved to see other people, like when stuff was coming at me; there was nobody that said 'Hey this is wrong. This is unbiblical the way this is happening.' So I don't know what, just like advocacy or stuff like that." Marshall expressed disappointment when his relationships soured in conflict: "I thought that their theology would overrule their culture, and it did not. I knew what their culture was. But I thought their theology would overrule, and it did not."

For some pastors, the feeling of betrayal even led to moments of spiritual crisis. Shelton poignantly describes such isolation: "The first question [is] 'What am I doing here?' That is not a one-time 'Ask and it gets answered.' It comes up. It repeats itself. The first time it confronts you, it's pretty loud. I will joke with people that Malcolm X, in one of his speeches when he's talking about America, he says we've been hoodwinked, we've been bamboozled, we've been led astray. And you get that feeling: 'God you tricked me.'"

Loss of Comfort and Sense of Home

Almost every pastor noted the loss of cultural comfort that came from being within the PCA. This loss of comfort also included a feeling of homesickness, whether for the Black Church or simply for a more comfortable cultural context.

> FERNANDO: I think majority culture needs to understand that African Americans . . . give up a lot to be part of this denomination. What usually happens is minority cultures sacrifice more than majority cultures when we do diversity ministry, when we do multicultural and cross-ethnic ministries.
>
> JIMMY: How am I going to help [other minority Christians] make a home, if I'm not even sure if I'm at home here? How am I going to create welcome for them here if I'm not even sure if I am welcomed here? That's the conundrum of the leader of color in the PCA. I'm not at home here, so how can I encourage other people to make a home here? How can I encourage them to lock in here if I am not sure that I am even stable here?
>
> MARSHALL: The PCA is a culture, not just a people of particular beliefs. It's very much a culture. And so as an African American, to come in to the PCA, you realize that you're walking into another culture.

ALEXANDER: When I came into the PCA, there was a cultural shock because the PCA has a particular kind of culture.

DESMOND: [Leaving for the PCA] was certainly something that we didn't want to do. [Another Black Reformed friend] and I had embraced among other things predestination and eternal security. So we knew we couldn't stay, because [our previous church] was a church that certainly believed in conditional election, that you could lose your salvation. So we left, not wanting to.

Two pastors articulated the blessing of experiencing worshiping in a comfortable cultural context. Thomas worshiped with other Black Reformed men at a retreat and was struck by how refreshing it was. Anthony experienced a PCA church successfully incorporating various forms of worship to appeal to the inner-city congregants in attendance:

THOMAS: Now, not just my mind or kind of American cultural identity has resonance with this, but my *Blackness*. I didn't have to check my Blackness. And these guys were just sharp. And there was a Black idiom in the preaching, it was just something . . . I felt at home. You know, you always long to be culturally at home and you get used to not being at home. I think this is the 'du Bois double consciousness.' We just always know we're not quite American. So I expect that in church, I expect that at work, at school, you just kind of expect that. There's a sense in which you're leaving your cultural comfort when you're going to a place like the PCA. So when I [went to that retreat], I saw that it doesn't have to be that way. I don't have to opt out of cultural comfort in order to receive these rich teachers.

ANTHONY: You also had more of a contemporary style for folks who were used to that, but then we also tried to mix in more of an urban feel, considering where we were. So the style was very fluid, very eclectic, trying to mirror the makeup of that particular church at that time. We had to keep in mind that we had a ton of youth there. So that also drove a lot of how worship went.

Even though some had these positive experiences, Shelton's remarks capture the feeling of most of my interviewees: "I would much rather be in a situation that was more comfortable culturally."

Loss of Connection with the Black Church

For some, the sense of loss was explicitly tied to the Black Church of their upbringing. For those who were raised in or had connections with the Black

Church, membership in the PCA meant loss. Some articulated a loss of comfort with the worship service:

> BRIAN: But eventually I began to notice that it was all White. The worship was different. It wasn't like the worship I grew up in.
>
> DESMOND: Being at the church of God felt like being home with your family worshiping. Now granted, there were about a thousand other family members with me worshiping. But it felt like family. Being at [a prominent Presbyterian Church], when I first got there, it really more felt like I was in a classroom lecture. It felt like I was back in college, in the sense that I was going to my sociology lecture, my psychology lecture, and there were just a bunch of people there, and we were there to hear the same thing and then get up and leave.

Others articulated a loss of history and ministry opportunities:

> FERNANDO: My wife, she grew up in the historical Black Church and I knew her marrying me meant giving up a lot. That means she was never ever going to be in the historical Black Church again, because of my calling, and that's what you stand to give up, for my wife who was in the historical Black Church since she was in diapers. Her church is over 100 years old. Her grandmother was part of the founding generation of that church. So saying goodbye to that history was hard.
>
> JIMMY: [Before] I had left the Black Church, I was on staff at a very influential Black Church, like nationally speaking . . . Through a kindness of the Lord and through friendship . . . I ended up coming on staff at that church, but that was simultaneously happening as we got to know [an influential PCA member]. I ended up having an opportunity [in the PCA] and I took it. I had stopped all of my effort to network and all of the stuff that happens, relationship-building, networking, I'd stopped doing that.
>
> DESMOND: When I was in [the previous church] there was no question that there was a place for me there. Had I remained a man called to the gospel with Arminian theology, had I remained committed to conditional election, committed to conditional assurance, there would be no question. I would never ever question there's a place for me [there] . . . to fulfill the calling I believe God gave to me and to be at home doing so, to be my full authentic self, in terms of how I preach and minister and serve, no doubt.

Two pastors described their theological journey away from the Black Church as moving from growing disdain to longing for home.

> SHELTON: You go through a process typically of having a disdain for the Black Church, which is not healthy. And so you actually have to come back around to actually appreciating how God has worked in a Black Church context, and valuing that. So what am I doing in here? Well God has put me here. Where else am I going to go? I'm not going to go anywhere. Because of this passion, this holy discontent, I can't go back to an all Black Church context. I don't fit . . . That's what I'm doing here, because in some senses I am a misfit.

> MARTIN: There was a period that you go through when you're learning Reformed theology . . . there's an arrogance phase to that, where you're looking down on the Black Church that I grew up with. For a little while, like oh, you know that theology was so weak and terrible and liberal and all this stuff. And then there's a period where you stop being so arrogant. Like, the problem wasn't so much the theology: it was you. You were dead in your transgressions and sins and close minded, and you learn to appreciate your heritage more, and celebrate the things from that heritage. And you don't want to lose those things. That's kind of the phase I went through. So you love the PCA and think, 'Oh man this is awesome. It's so much better than what I grew up with.' And then you're like, 'No it isn't. And man, I really miss the things I grew up with and I celebrate those things. And is there a way to bring things together?'

EXPERIENCING CULTURAL CONFLICT AND THEOLOGICAL ISOLATION

Cultures in Conflict

Often, the isolation that starts with cultural preferences—including preaching style, music preference, and worship expression—progresses from a sense of loss to a sense of dissonance. This cultural conflict takes place at multiple levels. First, some interviewees expressed a growing cultural tension as congregants in White PCA churches or students in seminary:

> BRIAN: Going to potlucks and covered dish. I didn't know what covered dish was. The foods were strange, so I had to get used to

eating foods that were different; and as long as I was willing to conform to White culture it worked.

SHELTON: You get a *de facto* message that says White is right. The *de facto* message is that White European theological work is the standard for good theology. No one comes out and says that, but that's what happens. Because you're learning, you're like a sponge eating the stuff up, and you're growing, but there is no *cultural* connection.

MARSHALL: My heroes were not White when I came to the PCA. So I'm not looking for White heroes. My heroes were African Americans. You know, our cultural heritage.

FERNANDO: I did not care for the music . . . They didn't culturally understand me . . . Most of the brothers and sisters that end up leaving, it's not over theology; it's over the cultural dynamics of dominant culture/subdominant culture stuff.

DESMOND: I was not looking to go to a mixed church. I wasn't looking to go to an overwhelmingly White Church that has worship so much different than what I came from.

THOMAS: The PCA really is a white-collar, suburban, White, fairly full of middle-class/upper-middle-class world. So that's transferable. I think a Black person going to First Pres in [a Southern city] is going to feel the same going to First Reformed in [a Northern city]. I visited one of these suburban First Pres type churches before and I was completely culturally alienated.

A second level of cultural conflict came as these Black ministers encountered White congregants resistant to their expressions of ministry. Martin and Desmond described ministry in majority-White contexts, while Marshall described his experience when dealing with White congregants in a more inner-city church:

MARTIN: [This] came up with some of my preaching. That was humbling also, but there were people that had a real problem with the style of preaching. Here is an example: at [my former church] one of things they do is a pastoral evaluation after the first year. They take a survey of the whole congregation and then we review it together. So, somebody wrote in there, like, I think it's inappropriate when he uses Black vernacular in his preaching.

DESMOND: There's my cultural expressions. In terms of how I preach, in terms of the examples I use, in terms of how a greater percentage of Black people may worship.

> MARSHALL: You still come here with your music, wanting someone preaching to you in a way that satisfies whatever. The worship service has gone pretty much like it would if you put it in some gentrified neighborhood or a White neighborhood.

A third level of cultural conflict involved minority pastors attempting to welcome other minorities into the congregation. One pastor, André, who ministers in a largely White congregation situated near a significant Black population in the city, describes the reactions his church gets from visiting minorities:

> ANDRÉ: We do have a lot of African Americans that show up to visit our church and never stay. They visit and I know I'll get together with them and talk, like: Yeah, can't stand your music. Yeah, can't stand the order of service and stuff like that. I think those are cultural things that make it difficult for minority pastors.

Racial Isolation: Experience and Articulation of Racial Dynamics

All of the pastors noted how they experienced race differently than the majority culture. This included self-identity: many noted how much race is a part of their every-day thinking. These pastors were not ubiquitous in their articulation of the precise cultural mechanics of race (as shown in the following section), but they were of one mind when it came to the impact racial realities had on their daily lives.

> FERNANDO: One of the things, when it comes to African Americans, is that there's not a day that I get up and I don't think about race. That it doesn't go through my mind. But for majority culture, you don't have to see those dynamics. In reality, you don't have to grow up and think about being White. I grew up thinking about being Black.

> BRIAN: The thing that White people don't realize is that Black people are *preoccupied* with race. I've said this before. I wake up in the morning: I'm Black. I work my day, I'm Black. And when I go to bed at night, I'm still Black.

> ANDRÉ: I do identify as Black, because that's just who I am, and I think that's my identity, my God-given identity. I think I should celebrate that: being a Black man.

ALEXANDER: As a Black minister pastoring to a majority-White congregation, you always ask yourself, if you have an idea, and that idea does not succeed, you can say two things: 'Oh, that was an awful idea,' or, 'I wonder if it didn't succeed because I'm Black.' No matter what you do that's always the second question.

SHELTON: You cannot help, in America, but think in racial terms in some shape. There's a filter that everything passes through.

FERNANDO: Put yourself in a situation where you're the minority. One of the moms was concerned because her daughter is one of the only White girls in the class. And I told my friend, 'Welcome to my world. That's what it's like for me all of the time.' It's always so. If you are a majority culture when you go into an environment where you're the only White person, that feeling you get, it's a feeling I get all the time. That's the feeling—feeling and realizing that not many people here look like you. So you feel a certain way. That's the feeling I feel. So when you put yourself in that context and you begin to identify, 'So that's what it feels like to be a minority.' In that situation, you realize you're White.

MARSHALL: We have to play that game all week long. And now I have to go to church on Sunday and play the same thing. Think about it: Whites don't change on Sunday. Even a multicultural church. They don't change. Now take African Americans, they go to a multicultural church and they'll be just as quiet. Go home to one of their parties and see how quiet they are. They tend to assimilate anyway when they're in that setting . . . Most of us code switch; that's just part of what you do.

In addition to these experiences, these leaders also noted that when they voiced their experience, it was met with confusion or frustration from Whites. Many noted that simple lack of cultural intelligence among congregants was partially to blame.

ANDRÉ: Almost 90 percent of our congregation did not know that there was an African American community that was just coming across the train [tracks]. I just came face to face with the reality of the racial divide.

FERNANDO: They have good intentions but they lack the know-how; they lack the cultural intelligence. That would be something I would encourage my majority-culture brothers and sisters to seek out: cultural awareness, cultural intelligence . . . Grow in that area, because it is really hard to love people who are different than you if you don't know anything about their culture.

JIMMY: Until we get good at loving in the places that are historically hard for American Western Christians to love in, and until we get good at dismantling the theological idolatries and the anthropological idolatries that are inherent in our way of thinking about the faith, it is going to handicap our missional efforts in this globalizing society.

THOMAS: So I don't really feel the race card—it's more cultural intelligence or racialization—that's more the issue. So we all just ran into some cultural troubles and issues. There is a danger in valuing race in an illegitimate way because of what it is. There's [also] a danger in devaluing it. I think we do need to just be racial realists that go, 'Yes, race is a proxy for a larger social dynamic and historical reality.'

THOMAS: I do think in a majority-minority situation, majority-culture White leaders have more anxiety about racism than the minorities do, because we just kind of live with racial realities. I think when you don't live with it, and when you feel like you have liabilities at stake . . . I just think there's a lot of fear. There's a lot of White people who have fear of saying the wrong thing, of not showing the proper politically correct speech . . . You guys have so much anxiety and fear about that kind of stuff, that you're going to mess up and it's going to end your career. Stuff we don't have as much. So anyway, often what that does is it makes it impossible to talk about the real issues, the real problem. It becomes impossible to say, 'Look I'm for you, but here's a thing you don't get.' When you say that, when you say X, you actually make us feel [pause] you actually create an unsafe emotional environment for minorities.

ALEXANDER: From a technical sense you can never take away from somebody's culture. A culture is formed early on and once that culture is embedded, that tends to be who you want to be, the way you process the world. But what you could do is you can add to a culture, and in fact what we call cultural assimilation is just you adding to your culture so much that your original culture doesn't inform so much what you do.

ANTHONY: The question for me is: Are they being listened to, and not necessarily just listened to, but is the advice being put into practice? I think that's where a lot of the disconnect has been. It's not enough simply to say we've been given an opportunity to give our piece and our thoughts and our feelings, which will sometimes run contrary to what the dominant culture in the PCA experiences or feels comfortable with. But for me, I would feel far more supported if much of what has been communicated will be put into practice.

Clearly, racial isolation is a significant force driving the sense of outsiderness these pastors experience. As they express the challenge of being Black in a majority-White Church, they show the painful divide between the racial experiences of Whites and Blacks, which cuts to the core of human identity. At the same time, because of these differences, the pastors have a unique vantage point into the dynamics of racial culture. They articulate a highly nuanced, culturally intelligent view of race in America, a view that offers rich insight for Whites, if they will listen.

Worldview Isolation: Interpretation of History, Dynamics of Oppression, and Cultural Events

Isolation also came from differences in thinking about race. For these pastors, disagreement over the proper interpretive lens for history, culture, and events became a major source of conflict. The way Black history shaped their identities increased the sense of alienation from the larger church culture:

> BRIAN: A lot of it has to do with our story. And the pain that we go through as individuals, our identity. And the fact that [after the Civil War] Whites didn't want to make Blacks on par with them in terms of the eldership: ruling elders and teaching elders.
>
> DESMOND: Bringing it all to the table; being able to say I can reference my history. And yes, I recognize that if I reference my history in this country . . . it makes some of you uncomfortable, because you can't be the hero. I know you have a problem with that. (I'm not saying you specifically; I'm saying you in general.) That's why, for example, when you want to talk about examples of God's faithfulness and God's people's faithfulness in the face of adversity, and you go back to the 1960s, you always talked about Christians in Communist countries. Why? Because you don't know what to do with the faithfulness of God to Black people, and God's people's faithfulness to the gospel and to God in the 60s during Civil Rights, because you're not the protagonist, and that's hard for you in general, as White people. You have to be the protagonist. You love to talk about that if you were in Nazi Germany in 1943 and you were hiding a group of Jews, of course it's okay to lie to the Gestapo. You don't want to talk

about how if you're in the barbershop in 1963, you know exactly who killed and strung the man up, you know exactly how they bragged about it, that you're not willing to tell the truth when the police officer comes and asks.

This conflict over the interpretation of history extended to church history as well. The racial history of the Reformed tradition led many pastors to automatically feel alienated. They had to wrestle with the implications of Presbyterian history, both personally and in ministry practice, when trying to reach other people of color.

> SHELTON: In seminary, I remember taking Church History: Reformation to the present day. They asked for feedback. I said if I did not know it experientially, I would not know from this class that there was actually a Black Church in America. We covered Reformation to the present day, and there is not one mention of the Black Church experience, the value of the Black Church, nothing. And I realized that it is because in part, it's not an intentional hatred, it is an ignorance. Sometimes I would say maybe a willful ignorance, but it is an ignorance.
>
> MARSHALL: I don't use the word Reformed because it doesn't mean anything to African Americans. I talk about us being covenantal, because African Americans understand that because they relate it to community. That's somebody else's vocabulary. That's another culture.
>
> SHELTON: (When talking about planting a Presbyterian church specifically aimed at minority Christians) They were distinctly not going to name the church Presbyterian, because it was seen as a barrier for people, the people they were trying to reach.

As mentioned above, a unique difference among my sample of pastors regarded place of birth. Shelton and André illustrate the unique differences between African American Blacks and Blacks born in other countries:

> SHELTON: Knowing your history of America, being Black in this country and—when it comes to Africans, this is different when it comes to Africans, first- or second-generation Africans who immigrate here. That wouldn't be a barrier to them, because you have a different experience, you haven't been or grown up racialized, where everything is codified in terms of race in your experience, so this is particular to an African American context.
>
> ANDRÉ: I know I was more accepted in the PCA than most African Americans that grew up here because of where I'm from. And so I feel like [people from my country] are more accepted

in America than the Black people in America for various reasons. One of them being history—I'm detached from the history of America in so many ways. And so you're talking about slavery and the civil rights movement and all of that. So just because I don't have that particular history, I am [pause] less intimidating.

The relationship between history and oppression also became a contentious issue in their worldview isolation. As Desmond observed, "of course [another point of tension] is, how do I view race in this country?" By this, he means how these pastors articulated the struggle of race in America. There was some difference in this sample of pastors on this point. Some noted how the majority culture generally did not see systems of oppression or injustice. One pastor noted how much he struggled with the current cultural understanding of race exclusively in terms of oppression, while another spoke freely about dynamics of oppression. Others simply noted that the shared history of the Black community created a sense of communal connection for them that was lacking in and misunderstood by Whites. Three excerpts from interviews with Brian, Terrance, and Thomas show how these brothers work for accuracy and precision in their articulation of the relationship between race and culture:

> BRIAN: But the Builders and the Boomers think of sin in individualistic terms and not systemic. But that is beginning to change. As Christians become minorities, I think it's beginning to change. We were a so-called Christian country, and so you don't think of the systemic, because you're part of the system. You're blind to the systemic oppression when you are in the majority, because you are the oppressor. And so, you think everything is individualistic. And I don't think it was malicious; I just think it was blindness.
>
> TERRANCE: I feel like my own eyes have been opened more and more to the systemic kind of, I hate to say, that kind of White privilege. You know, it's not always just White priv— [pause] It is White privilege, but it's the lens through which ministry is looked at by the majority culture, and they don't realize that it's their culture driving it.
>
> THOMAS: We had a Black president for eight years. Here's why [it is significant for Black people]—not because this guy has Black skin, [but] because what that represents is a group of people that historically have experienced marginalization, oppression, being able to break through in the most significant way possible . . . The color is representative—the color is a proxy for cultural progress. So in a sense, acknowledging my Blackness

says we're making progress in the ability to relate, connect with, allow, enter in, and be influenced by the cultural perspective/person that we normally aren't influenced by or make room for; so it's a proxy for a larger point, historical point.

Even when these pastors have different formulations for cultural forces like systemic oppression or privilege, their analysis was driven by their experiences of being Black in America.

A third point of worldview isolation is the interpretation of cultural events, such as the deaths of Trayvon Martin or Michael Brown. Black pastors tended to interpret these events with more significance than their White congregants:

> DESMOND: I was trying to be instructive to the congregation I was serving at that time, just to explain: this is why you're seeing this outcry and this backlash, so let me instruct you how to engage. And it was just rejected roundly. It was rejected roundly, because it was said, 'This has nothing to do with the gospel; this has nothing to do with what our church is about or should be about. This is a strictly political thing that has been politicized by the media and other race-baiters. We have no connection to what happened in Florida because we're in [a different city]. And you don't really have a connection to Trayvon Martin. He is not a family member of yours; you don't know him. This is completely out of line.' Whereas in the Black Church, it would be completely defended. That's something that would have been mentioned in every Black Church. It's not something that would have been mentioned in a White Church, and that's because in the Black community, you have not only this shared history, there is this covenantal connectivity that—whatever I know about Trayvon and this person, what he was doing there and how this started—I just recognize that it could have been my son. I remember President Obama catching a lot of flack for that. He said, 'If I had a son, he would look like Trayvon.' People were saying he's race-baiting and all that, but he was touching something within the collective consciousness of our community. When something tragic happens in that sense to a White person, it's almost disconnected. But when that happens to a Black person there is this connection. So that's what's mentioned in a Black Church. And so, there is difficulty in ministering in a White Church because if you mention it, there is pushback. And that happened to me personally.
>
> MARTIN: And we're talking about those issues [like the Michael Brown shooting], some people in our church would feel

like, 'Oh no, this is identity politics. This is getting away from the gospel. This is the slippery slope of liberalism.' And anytime you raise these issues, they're like, 'You're bringing up stuff that's extra-biblical.' There's a nontrusting [attitude]. Or I would bring up the examples of, like the talk I'd have with my sons when they're driving . . . I shared that with our church, because I want them to know. And people feel like you're shaming White people. People say that stuff. And there are people that left our church because of that stuff.

When bringing up these cultural events, these pastors face criticism and rebuke from their White congregants or other White elders in the denomination. Backlash over a pastor's view of race, history, and cultural events only leads to more exhaustion and more isolation.

Experiencing Paternalism, Marginalization, and Microaggressions

"Our experience was one of always feeling like outsiders, always feeling like minorities, paternalism. Gracious acceptance, although a desire for conformity. Be like us. The sense has always been a tolerance." This was Brian's summary of the Black experience in the PCA. Every pastor interviewed had numerous examples of inequality, whether in the form of paternalism, marginalization, or microaggressions.

Paternalism

Many pastors experienced paternalism in their relationships with other White leaders or congregants. Some felt they were never on equal footing with Whites in ministry. Others felt White congregants or pastors were motivated by a sense of guilt, not the genuine desire for relationship. Marshall described this feeling as "we'll get one or two of y'all, or three or four or five of y'all to pastor us, that way we'll feel good about not being racist anymore." Others experienced paternalism by feeling pigeonholed by their race—as if their only meaningful contribution could be on the topic of race. Still others experienced paternalism when asked to represent the entirety of their race.

> FERNANDO: There are so many different versions of what it means to be American based upon our experiences . . . I think there's a temptation to think that maybe all African Americans are the same—we're not the same. Even within African American

culture there are cultural differences. I grew up in [the South East]. I didn't grow up in South Central LA; a brother in South Central LA and myself, we're Black but culturally we're different. Country [Southern state] and the streets of LA are two different worlds. And so, we're different. Our worlds are different. So just knowing that takes culture intelligence and realizing that there's so much diversity even within Black culture—the only way you know that is that you got to build relationships with people.

ANTHONY: It's important to reach out to a good number of the African Americans because we're not all a monolith in terms of our experiences, in our ministry experiences, where we're gifted. Because like I said, there are African Americans who are in more affluent churches and then there are some who are in less affluent churches—our responses are going to be based on that. And I think some of the dangers in times past are that they've taken opinions from just a handful and assume that what they communicated represents every other African American.

SHELTON: By welcoming us in and earnestly desiring to listen to our perspective, to value and say, we're not only interested in talking to you when it comes to race, as if you should be pigeon-holed, being an expert in what to do when it comes to race.

DESMOND: There seems to be a willingness to quickly pigeon-hole and assess someone whose issues on how they think about race don't line up with the Reformed majority.

JIMMY: I think recognizing that we need people of color to understand more than just race. It's everything. By virtue of my ordination as a Teaching Elder in this church, I have been deemed by the [Local] Presbytery as capable of speaking to the whole counsel of God, not just the issue of race.

THOMAS: That was a bad racial experience for me. But it didn't sour me on the PCA. What it soured me on was the racial hubris of urbane transformational PCA types. They think they get the diversity down. They really don't. They really bring their middle-class, suburban, White culture with them. That's OK—we all need to grow ... What's interesting is this is an American thing. The relationship with minorities that these churches have is very paternalistic. They have to do Mercy Ministries for all the poor kids; it's never an equal partnership. Seldom. So it's not a Black person with the same influence, status, power, same as the White person. It's always got to be, you know [pause] Use the word, people get offended. [pause] I just feel like so often the only model that works for people psychologically is a "plantation model" [laughter], not one where there's really a sense of people self-giving and sharing.

ANTHONY: The issue comes in when we have folks who might come in from out of our city to try to help, or folks that we reach out to for help, whether it's resources of whatever sorts. That's where the issues tend to come in . . . It's not necessarily intentionally trying to be hostile, but just a great deal of ignorance in terms of what the urban community is like. And there is this, not patriarchal, but there is this feeling that we're kind of an 'other' in the PCA, and not necessarily just because of the race, but where you're located, the type of ministry you're doing. And 'If you want our help then this is the way it has to be done,' even if it's not helpful to the community itself. So in this effort to maintain tradition or history, which is obviously affected by racial dynamics and economic dynamics, that has come off as very off-putting in terms of my interactions with certain churches and even certain people in the PCA.

JIMMY: I don't want to be overly prescriptive but I think that could show up in our desire to hire someone, not as a token and not as a mannequin—a 'diversity mannequin'—but someone who has something to teach us, and we are going to be humble enough to listen . . . We are not going to put the burden of diversifying our congregation on that one person of color.

MARTIN: You have so many stories of guys who were the Great Black Hope and that even happened to me some. People expect you know it's like *Field of Dreams*—"If you hire them, they will come"—without changing anything else about the church. And it's always a disappointment for both.

Marginalization

Marginalization occurred as these pastors felt simply unwanted or unimportant. Desmond captured the feeling of marginalization when he described how the PCA seemed to treat him toward the beginning of his ministry, nearly 20 years ago: "The PCA wasn't looking for African American members or ministers. That simply was not in their vision. It was not malicious, 'We don't need you,' but it's like 'We don't really see that we need you. It's good that you're here. But we don't need you.'" As the following three quotes show, marginalization comes about largely through apathy, which suggests they are not wanted, that their ministries are unimportant, and that the issue of diversity is one that they must bear alone.

> DESMOND: [Refering to a prominent Presbyterian church] That simply was not in their vision . . . They were about 160, 170 years old. And they certainly had a good strong biblical witness in the city of [historic American city] but they didn't have an impetus. And they didn't seem to have a desire to expand that witness to various ethnic groups. . . . It was the same thing again within the PCA, and in our Presbytery.
>
> ANTHONY: We've asked folks who are in the upper echelons of the denomination, in terms of influence, to come to our communities, to come to our neighborhoods, spend time there, not just necessarily for a mission trip but come and just to witness and learn and see for themselves. And yet you don't really get people responding to those particular challenges, inviting our people, in churches like ours, to their cities, their churches, and things like that, just to witness and learn and fellowship. There are some of those, but it's almost as if, you know . . . we're not on equal footing so to speak. One is the project. The other is the project manager, so to speak.
>
> SHELTON: And I know that I'm going to have to fight to find ways and means of renewal that help me deal with the minority fatigue I know I'm going to experience . . . It's too heavy a load to carry, and actually we're not supposed to carry it by ourselves. We press into it, but it is necessary to have this commitment to the denomination because we have to communicate to our majority-culture brothers that they got to press this issue too. This is not simply 'our issue' to carry.

Microaggressions

Microaggressions consist of remarks, suggestions, or actions that implicitly undermine the minority's status, even if they initially sound well-meaning.[4] Significantly, almost every pastor I interviewed explicitly stated that these stories were outliers, not representative of their entire experience in the PCA. Moreover, these pastors attempted to read the experience through the

---

4. There are a few main manifestations of microaggressions: "intentionally and explicitly derogatory verbal or nonverbal attacks; . . . rude and insensitive subtle put-downs of someone's racial heritage or identity; and. . . , remarks that diminish, dismiss, or negate the realities and histories of People of Color" (see Yosso et al., "Critical Race Theory," 662).

lens of charity and grace, giving the people the benefit of the doubt whenever possible. Most of them would go on to say that their experience in the PCA has been good and is improving. Still, the emotional toll of receiving exclusionary comments adds up, as the question of race weighs on the imagination of the minority pastor. Alexander put it like this:

> If you are an African American or a Black man in a predominately White space, White Church or whatever, if somebody doesn't like you or somebody's treating you weird or different, there are two things you think about automatically. One is, 'Did I do something to offend this person? Is it just me as a person?' Or two, 'Is it because I'm Black?' I'm not saying that that's right, I'm just saying that's the extra step . . . As a Black person in a majority-White space, you have to go to the second level. I hate to go there, but experience has taught me that this is still an issue.[5]

The following anecdotes are organized into two categories: exclusionary comments coming from congregants and exclusionary comments coming from church officers, whether deacons or elders.

> DESMOND: People will begin to throw out what I would say is a sort of a test balloon. 'So what do you think of Jesse Jackson? What do you think of Al Sharpton? Why do all Black people vote Democrat? Don't they know that it was Democrats who were the ones who were pushing segregation?'
>
> BRIAN: I had one White person who said he thought we were going to plant a Black middle-class church, and he said we would do it the same way we would do a White Church plant, 'Because Black people are just dark White people.' Black people are just dark people, and we're the same, and one's just dark. We do the same thing, our values are the same, my thoughts are the same, we are the same, it's just that one is dark and one is not. You are constantly pushing up against this perception that you are the same as me. 'I don't think of you as Black.' You get that.
>
> JIMMY: I feel disenfranchised, like my voice doesn't matter, when I feel like my heroes don't matter, when I hear people say no one from my ethnic world has ever made a positive contribution to theology or Christianity. Those kind of things. The hero worship of Southern Presbyterian fathers, those kinds of things are subtle ways of saying, 'You are always going to be an outsider

---

5. This is significant coming from Alexander, who of the twelve interviewees, was the most positive about his experience in the PCA, describing it thusly: "it's just been a joy and a blessing all the way through."

here.' So it makes it difficult to call other people to enter into something where you feel threatened there.

WB: Do you feel like people say 'Your heroes have not made a positive contribution . . .'

J: I have heard that verbatim. I actually heard someone say those very words to me. 'Y'all sing good. That's about the only contribution that you have made.' He verbally articulated that vantage point.

THOMAS: The executive director said, 'You have a sharp tongue, you're a big guy with a deep voice and a sharp tongue; you gotta be careful.' I heard 'big Black guy—scary.' That's one of those things, when you're in that culture, you just have to adapt.

MARSHALL: One White guy actually told me, [referring to other previous Black pastors] he said, 'You know, their style, I can understand it, but your style is so different.' Now understand, people will say I'm a pretty good exegete. So, basically, you're just talking about a little bit of, you know . . . I tend to be animated, crack a little joke, whatever the case may be. And I said, 'That's so interesting. Here you are moving to this all-Black community to minister to these poor Black people and yet when you get a Black preacher that acts like, walks like, and talks like the people you say you want to be "incarnational" with, you're talking about his style. Because basically you want to come into this Black community and pat yourself on the back about, "You down here in the hood to minister to Black people." But you don't want anything that resembles the community from this hood to be your spiritual authority. Your White racism still tells you that you are dominant. And if you're going to be gracious enough to come down here and serve me, I ought to at least make you feel good about it.' It's paternalism, at the least.

ANDRÉ: People have questioned my legality in America. People have questioned whether I could preach, and I kid you not, this was a letter I received from a congregant asking, basically telling me that I could not preach the gospel in America because I was not born here and I do not understand the American history. And, so, to him, for me to be able to share the gospel and properly preach the gospel, I needed to go back, I needed to learn American history. And people asked me just before I became a pastor if my goal was to bring, quote, 'those Black people' to church.

MARTIN: I'll tell you one anecdote. We had an affiliate for Habitat for Humanity at the church I worked with. There'd be a ton of volunteers, a lot them from PCA churches in the area, predominantly White. I remember we were at this house dedication and someone said, 'Hey this is my first year at [the church]; this is the pastor for [the church]' and the guy, White guy, looks and he's like, 'You're the pastor? Really?' And I said, 'Yeah.' And he says, 'Are you ordained?' I said, 'Yeah, yeah I'm ordained,' and he walked away. And then there's a White guy with me from our church and he's like, 'Did you hear what he said?' [Laughter] Because what he was asking was like, 'How can you be ordained and you're Black? How could you get ordained in the PCA?' Like that's impossible. That's what he was getting at. And my friend got it. There was much more like that when I was early on.

ALEXANDER: It's been overwhelmingly positive, so let me tell you a story that hasn't been positive. And let me just add that I don't allow this particular experience to color the overwhelmingly positive experience . . . [When I was interning at a church in the South] there would be a lady who every time I went to preach she would stand up and leave. Right before I started preaching or if I came and she saw me and [the senior pastor] wasn't there she would leave. [When I told the pastor, he said] 'She's what you classically call a racist. She doesn't believe that a Black man should be preaching to her.' And then he proceeded to tell me there were several people in the congregation whose family had ties with the KKK and various organizations that resisted African Americans, on school boards and different things like that. I said 'Well you know this woman is denying herself the means of grace because of me. Isn't that cause for church discipline?' He said he understood but he also wanted to deal with her in her weakness. And she said that she was aware that her behavior was sinful, but he said that she just couldn't bring herself to do that. She had been taught that. She'd been taught a particular way, that African Americans were not supposed to exercise authority over Whites . . . We still treated her with love . . . My wife and I prayed, and Jesus said in this life you'll have tribulation. And this was one tangible way we felt like we can show the love of Christ, because the Bible says pray for those that hate you, and treat those well that may or may not be as kind to you. We viewed it as that, but it was still difficult. Because we saw the way she interacted with everybody else and then with us it was [pause] it was a noted difference.

TERRANCE: Our worship has been blended. And when we say blended, we mean really blended. We sing some songs in

Spanish, we sing some songs that are, you know, R&B/Gospel. We sing some songs that are Chris Tomlin stuff. I mean, we're all over the place . . . because we want to reflect the people who are in our building. But one time, one of my elders said: 'I just want to make sure we're going to stay blended because [pause] we're not going to [pause] I almost feel like we're becoming a Black Church.' And I was kinda like, 'Okay?' Now I know this guy. He is a sweet man. He's been great. But my thought was, 'Okay? So, what if we did? What would be wrong with that? What are you saying there, when you make that statement? You know, because my Black brothers and sisters, if they just heard you say that, bro, you're no longer their elder anymore; you're racist.'

ALEXANDER: When they had the racial reconciliation overture, I think it's 2016 GA in Mobile. I went to lunch with [several folks on the Overtures committee]. They just said, 'Listen we cannot have an African American in our church.' I mean, it was candid. They were just being honest. Like if an African American came to our church that would be an issue. There were other people that said, you know, 'We would welcome in African Americans, but it'd be a problem if we brought one on staff. It'd be an even bigger problem for them if they were on the pastoral staff.' I had people who said that they themselves were still struggling because of the way they grew up with racism, or feeling like the African American culture or Black culture is inferior to Anglo culture.

ALEXANDER: After a Bible study, a deacon came up to me and said, 'You know, it just breaks my heart, all of this back-and-forth about African Americans. I don't understand why God just didn't make everyone the same color.' And then I said immediately, 'Yeah. It'd be great if we're all Black,' and the look on his face was priceless, because he didn't have to say it, right? It was obvious that he was saying, it would be great if God made everybody White.

Pressure to Conform

Paternalism, marginalization, and microaggressions came with a pressure to conform to White culture. Multiple pastors acknowledged a sense that they needed to adopt White culture in order to be fully accepted. Thomas and Brian shared what it felt like as Black congregants in White PCA churches.

THOMAS: And it was culturally very difficult from that point on. It's always a little bit difficult when you're a 'onesie'; you are always in survival mode. So, I was really just kind of in survival mode, do what you can, because it's just different code, a different language you have to operate in. You have to live in double consciousness. You have to adapt to the majority culture; it doesn't adapt to you.

BRIAN: Eventually I began to realize that unless I conform to White culture, I really was not being accepted. I was not being accepted as a Black man. So, because I was [initially] accepted in that culture, I tried to conform to that culture.

The pressure to assimilate focused on multiple pressure points, and individuals felt judged if they fell short on these pressure points: how they acted or talked in worship—specifically, how they preached—who they lauded as heroes, and what they believed about race:

DESMOND: Another difficulty obviously is the idea that people will say, 'Well we certainly would want more Black people. Do you think we should have them?' But the undercurrent is 'as long as they're willing to be like us.' And by that, it's meant, as long as they're willing to think about the issue of race the way we think about the issue of race. As long as they are willing to not only conform their expression of worship, but why they worship that way, to us.

DESMOND: I had to make it clear that I didn't think like they did on race. There is the assumption that because your theology has changed, your view with respect to race has changed, and so people talk to you as if you're a Black political conservative just because you are a Black theological conservative . . . And those are almost sort of trial test balloons to say, 'Where is he? I just need to make sure.'

MARSHALL: You say you wanna be diverse, but why do I have to use your words, walk like you, talk like you, preach like you?

ANTHONY: I really enjoy the freedom and the opportunity to do the type of work that I'm doing in an urban context. Whereas if I was forced to assimilate or come into a neighborhood such as mine and make it look more traditionally Presbyterian, that would not only be a problem for me, it would be a problem for the community that I'm called to serve.

MARSHALL: I'm trying to smooth it off a little bit just to be heard. But on the same token, if I smooth it off too much [pause]

What I tell people is I've got degrees from your institutions, I know how you talk, I know how you write. Don't you think you could move a little bit toward me? Why is it always me making myself palatable for you?

ANDRÉ: If you want to be a part of the PCA, whether you're a pastor, whether you're an assistant pastor, or a music director, or just a congregant, you know you've got to do several things. First of all, you've got to believe this stuff that we believe, and then you're going to behave the way we behave. And then maybe you will belong, if we let you in.

What is the cost of succumbing to the pressure to assimilate? As Fernando and Marshall demonstrate, the cost is both existential and ministerial: existentially, the sense of self gets lost, and ministerially, pastoral effectiveness is sacrificed.

FERNANDO: We won't ever be fully in Black culture again, and we're not going to just assimilate into majority-culture way of life. . . I found myself adopting majority-culture view of things, and not being around my other African Americans. I think it wasn't healthy for me . . . Looking back I missed out, because struggling with identity, worshiping in a majority culture, hating my culture, hating the Black Church, thinking the majority culture was right about everything. I was in this world of no longer being in Black culture but find myself almost being assimilated into majority culture.

MARSHALL: We used to send guys out who could preach just as good as [a prominent Black minister] could, some better, but they couldn't plant a successful church. And I kept asking the question, 'Why?' When they came out [of the White context] they were condescending toward Black people. How do you expect to grow a Black Church when basically all your references are White? All your heroes are White. That doesn't work. That's like going to a White Church and now you're quoting Martin Luther King, or the founding fathers of the Black movement. Nobody would care. They're not their heroes. They're not their cultural heroes; they're not their religious heroes. Most Blacks . . . I mean, I was surprised, even the pastors . . . they didn't even know the Black evangelicals whose shoulders they stood on.

Restricted Sense of Identity: "I can't be my full self."

The sum total of these experiences led to a restricted sense of identity, an unfulfilled longing to bring one's full self into the ministry. As Terrance said: "I didn't feel like I could be myself." The threat presents a challenging choice: give in to the restricted self, and possibly lose self-identity, or exercise your full self and lose your place in the community. As at the start, these pastors face loss either way.

Those who give in to the restricted self suffer from identity confusion, especially as younger pastors. This experience is most poignantly expressed through Fernando's experience during his early years in ministry: "On the inside, culturally, I was still confused, just not knowing who I was . . . felt like I was a little more of an Uncle Tom, not really Black anymore, because I was no longer in Black culture. I was in majority culture all the time now."

Those who struggled against the restricted self were faced with other forms of loss: loss of status, of friends, of positions, or of ministry peace, as Desmond described: "When you are your authentic self, you can have so much pushback. You can have so much resistance. You can be viewed with such suspicion."[6] Marshall described the frustration of losing church members if he refused to conform:

> You'll lose White people who said they want a Black person, a Black leadership. 'We [want] a strong Black pastor.' No, you don't, you don't even know what that means . . . Because guess what? You're not used to sitting under a Black man—[you want] a Black man that makes you feel good about your culture, and I'm not trying to make you feel good about your culture. Guess why? 'Cause I feel good about mine. See, that's multicultural. You feel good about yours. And let me feel good about mine. But that's difficult to do. I think in America it's difficult, just given our history.

Brian faced the possible loss of friends if he gave in to the restricted self: "But as time went on, I realized I was alone and that my White Church didn't understand me. I understood it but they didn't understand *me*. They didn't get *me*. I think as long as I was willing to hold my breath on that it was okay."

As both Desmond and André articulate, this struggle over the whole self ultimately impacts ministry effectiveness:

---

6. Desmond would go on to say he feels that this dynamic is changing, that there are more places now in the PCA where he would be able to bring his whole self into the ministry.

DESMOND: There is also the difficulty [of] not being able to bring your whole self into the picture. And by that I simply mean that as a Black person, can you bring that to your ministry? There are certain things that I have experienced. There are certain issues within my community that I would bring up in ministry, in sermons, maybe even as illustrations. In the Black Church, it would be natural and picked up immediately. Many times, within the Reformed context, it's resisted. It makes it difficult to bring your whole self as you try to serve, and as you try to minister.

ANDRÉ: If I'm going to serve my church well, if I'm going to love my people well, I can't pretend to be someone else. I've got to be me. When I preach, I actually had some people leave the church because they thought I was too passionate. I was like, 'Well do you want me to preach and be myself and just be who I am?' And they said yes. And I asked, 'Have you ever had a chat with me about the gospel? And did you see how animated and excited I was about it? That's who I am.' So when I stand in the pulpit, I don't act to be someone else . . . I don't hold back. So let me be myself, so that I can love you well and I can minister to you well.

These pastors face a tight-rope walk between faithfulness to their God-given self and faithfulness to gospel ministry, all while enduring the pressure to conform to the majority culture. This conflict is profound: Do you give into the cultural straitjacket and exist within a restricted sense of self, or do you express yourself and face pushback, job loss, and ministerial crisis? For White-majority pastors, ministry is difficult enough without these competing tensions. But for outsiders on the inside, ministry includes these existential stressors on top of normal wear-and-tear of the ministry. How does this feel?:

MARTIN: Part of the experience is feeling like there has to be an apologetic when you're bringing these things up, like you're saying, 'No, I'm not getting away from the gospel. No this isn't an addition . . . [I have to] help people see that this is actually an outworking of the gospel from Scripture.' So there's kind of a built-in apologetic that you realize you have to give. And sometimes that's tiring.

WB: Tiring because . . .

M: Because you just can't just be . . . you're worried about making a mistake, because you're going to be classified as a liberal, or a heretic, or a militant, or something, or getting away from the gospel.

7

Learning to Thrive

AFTER AN INITIAL WELCOME, these pastors uniformly experienced a painful reality: they were viewed as outsiders. Though they were members in good standing, time and again individuals and systems failed to fully welcome them as members in one way or another. This led every pastor to a fork in the road: Stay, or leave? While some in their shoes have chosen to leave, these pastors chose to stay, learning to thrive in the face of these challenges by committing to the PCA, embracing a shared theological tradition, thinking strategically about the future, and adopting an outlook marked by gratitude.[1]

---

1. This theoretical category was originally titled "Becoming Culture-Changers." To gain descriptive precision, I bounced this title off one of my interviewees in a personal conversation after his interview. He expressed some concern that my original wording was too triumphalist. Based on this feedback, I chose instead to highlight the concept of thriving, which met with his approval. His response to my suggestion: "Yes, it is more like learning to thrive in a hostile culture."

> **Table 4: Learning to Thrive**
>
> Stage Three of the Journey
>
> 1. Committing to the PCA
>   * A providential calling
>   * A theological heritage
> 2. Embracing a shared biblical-theological tradition
> 3. Forming life-giving relationships
> 4. Thinking strategically about the future
>   * Developing networks for minority leaders
>   * Institutional focus (Agencies and leadership)
>   * Institutional focus (Resources and equipping)
>   * Local pastoral focus
> 5. Practicing gratitude

COMMITTING TO THE PCA

A Providential Calling

There is a clear sense of God's call as these pastors consider their presence in the PCA. They recognize God's sovereign choice in placing them here, which helps fuel their determination to stay and thrive within the PCA. Each of the twelve interviewees expressed a calling to the PCA, whether specifically in the language of call, or more generally in the sense of following God's will:

> FERNANDO: I sensed a call to ministry, to be in the PCA, to plant a cross-cultural church next to a historic Black community . . . The only thing I can draw from that is that it is the Holy Spirit, a calling from God. So I'm here because there's a calling from God.
>
> BRIAN: [When interacting with African Americans interested in coming into the PCA] I say, 'Why do you want to be in the PCA?' I quiz. And people who say, 'Sell me,' I say, 'I'm not going to sell you. If you don't feel called, please don't come.'
>
> DESMOND: God is at work. God is at work in our denomination. And I believe he will continue to be at work. I really do.
>
> JIMMY: When I look over the providence of the way in which the Lord got me here, I can't downplay that.

THOMAS: The fact is, there are some people who let race be the determining factor. The question to ask is, 'Am I called to minister here or not?' The question is not, 'Is he Black?,' but, 'Has God called him to minister here? Is the Spirit enabling him?' The Spirit doesn't know those kinds of distinctions, right?

SHELTON: Central to our theological commitment is the sovereignty of God. He determined the time and the seasons for all men, and the places. So if I believe that, okay God, what am I doing here? God put me here . . . This is where God has called me to be. [And then a] switch happened to me a couple of years ago, where I said, 'Okay, if I'm going to be in, I'm going to be all the way in.'

THOMAS: I always answer this the way [another Black PCA minister] answers it: it's a providential calling. I feel a sense of, 'Well, I've experienced God's providential direction.' I've tried to serve out in another world. Doors shut. PCA doors opened wide, like my current position. Doors just flew wide open for that. I didn't look for it. [Another] pastor met me at a conference; we talked. They made things open, all other things, doors opened relative to that, whereas I tried to knock on some other doors before, and nothing happens and there's just a sense of God saying—I'm not charismatic, obviously—but there's just a sense of calling, like, 'This is the world I want you in.' Providentially God has directed those steps just by opening and shutting this door.

MARSHALL: I'm definitely afraid of doing anything that's outside of God's will . . . This is the door he opened.

ANDRÉ: I think the Lord has called me to the PCA. I think that's really important . . . I do feel called to the PCA.

MARTIN: I think, ultimately, it's a sense of call that this is where we belong . . . it's been a sense of call to the PCA.

As seen in the quotes above, sensing God's call clearly empowers the ministry of these men in three ways: first, it enables them to endure the challenges of the denomination; second, it motivates them to commit deeply to the denomination; and third, it shapes a vision of their ministry.

This vision of ministry is twofold: first, some view their presence as revealing theological blind spots, thus working to help sanctify the whole denomination. As Brian articulated it, "I believe that God brings, and is bringing, African Americans into the PCA to open up our eyes. There's a blind spot. You are blind. We need the whole body of Christ to begin to see.

We all have blind spots. We are sinners. We are broken." Second, almost universally, these men view themselves as being a part of God's redemptive plan to bring the nations together as God's people. Jimmy's words sum up what many of the men said about their sense of call: "So I eventually worked through it, and became convinced that I could be a part of the solution by laboring in a world that needs to grow in this most important area; or I could not be a part of the solution, and I could go back to a place where everyone is like me [in the Black Church]."[2]

A Theological Heritage

Not only is their presence in the PCA due to God's calling, it is also a theological heritage. Two pastors in particular expressed how powerful it was to discover that there were Black Presbyterians in history going back to the Civil War. One pastor said that this revelation gave him a sense of having a right to be in the denomination. Another expressed that this knowledge finally freed him to say "fathers and brothers" when speaking at a denominational event:

> FERNANDO: I'm here because I have ancestors who are Presbyterian . . . When I was researching the history of African American Presbyterianism, realizing that my ancestors have been in Presbyterianism for 215 years, since 1807, the question I ask myself is, why did they persevere? In the denomination that really didn't want them there—the denomination that wouldn't speak out against slavery, the denomination . . . that had glimpses of some churches and others speaking out, but as a whole, they did not . . . I have a right to be here. This is a denomination of my Black forefathers and mothers. They paved the way for me to be here. So, it's a calling, and it's a right for me to be here, and I'm standing on their shoulders continuing the work that they have done. I feel like they will be proud of what is taking place in the PCA branch of Presbyterianism.
>
> SHELTON: From a history standpoint, one of the things that African Americans are now looking into is having to do research into the history of African American and Black Presbyterianism—the realization that we do have fathers in the faith in Presbyterianism. This was new for me, because until [recently], I never, never at any Presbyterian meeting or General Assembly,

---

2. This sense of playing a part in God's larger redemptive mission was so prevalent that it warranted its own theme, found below.

I've never said 'fathers and brothers.' I've always said 'brothers.' Just from an African American standpoint, it is hard to call a room full of White men fathers. I've got a father. So even our language or culture, you don't realize, a Black man to say 'fathers.' So, I said that for the first time this year, and I've been in the PCA [for many years]. And in part because, whether or not this is right, it's because I'm realizing there's a rich Black American Presbyterian history. There are fathers in the faith. We've got them. And we're just working on bringing that to the fore, and expressing that.

EMBRACING A SHARED BIBLICAL-THEOLOGICAL TRADITION

As noted above, as these men worked through their sense of calling, most landed on a profound insight: they are in the PCA because God is doing a redemptive work, knitting together a racially diverse people. Importantly, this insight has both biblical and Reformed theological foundations. On a biblical level, most pastors noted that the grand sweep of Scripture points toward diversity. This biblical insight motivated them to stick with the work of multicultural ministry; even while they may feel a sense of homelessness as outsiders, the biblical narrative helped them embrace their calling to minister outside of the Black Church. As well, because of the PCA's commitment to biblical theology, they felt they had the resources to win others to a similar vision through their preaching and teaching:

> ANTHONY: In my mind, the kingdom of God itself is diverse. And I would love to see the PCA become more diverse.
>
> TERRANCE: As long as you're helping move the ship, if you will, this big ship called the PCA—help move a little closer to God's vision, then we're making progress. It's all things being brought back to Christ under his lordship and I just can't imagine that's not ethnic, [that it] doesn't include ethnicity. I can't read Ephesians and think any different. There's just no way . . . all that to say, God wants to bring the nations back into being the people of God.
>
> SHELTON: I know my own heart passion to see the local church look like its community and its diversity, that unity in diversity, and diversity in unity, is a gospel imperative for the church of Jesus Christ.

FERNANDO: If this gets off the ground, it is going to really benefit the African American movement and overall PCA when it comes to looking more like Revelation 7.

ANDRÉ: I think this story of humanity is one story. Israel is not just another group of people. Israel is a reflection of who we are. We may have some different cultural things going on and stuff like that, but our history is a story of the fall. It's the story of God's redemption for humanity.

JIMMY: Race matters. Well how much does race matter? We know it matters because racialization is so real, it's in our face, so we know something's going on here, even if race is just a social construct. But we also know in the kingdom of God, we also know the way God works by his Spirit: race is relativized in light of union with Christ and our larger connection as a multiethnic, blood-bought, redeemed family. It's marginalized, but not irradicated; God made it—it's a beautiful thing, but it's put down. It's not this kind of leading thing that drives everything. But we know it's something, because even God is attentive to it in redemption, and you know 'from every tribe, nation,' there's an attentiveness to the diversity of people and how the gospel goes to all.

ALEXANDER: Don't question the will of God—I believe firmly that had sin not happened, all of us would have been varying colors. I don't necessarily think all of us would have been one color. I don't think multiple colors came as a result of sin.

DESMOND: I think first of all it's a biblical commitment. Reading through Scripture, it's become more and more clear to me... that it is Christ's intention to have a multiethnic, multicultural worshiping community that we call the church. And that is what he is doing through the gospel. And so for me to go back—well, I couldn't go back to the Arminian church anyway—but for me to just pull out and say, 'Well let's just start a Reformed Black Church,' would be unbiblical. There's that core biblical conviction: this is what God is doing through the gospel. Along with that, I'd say if God is doing this through the gospel, I should expect opposition from the enemy and from the evil one. I should not expect this to be easy... The PCA is committed to Scripture and so it's, again, conviction... If asked, 'Okay. Let me walk you through the Old Testament. Let me walk you through the book of Acts and walk you through the book of Ephesians.' You will come and you [might] say, 'I never looked at those books in that manner before. But now that you've done that, maybe I don't agree with all of what you're saying, but I can see where you're coming from and where it's biblical.' And so, if I believe I'm in a biblical denomination, that says they stand on the word of God, then they will be willing to make those changes. And I think I've seen the fruit of that.

WB: Why not start an African American Presbyterian denomination?

BRIAN: All of our attempts to start churches have all been [pause] God has ruined our plans . . . I think God wants us to be multiethnic. [Recently there was] an African American Presbyterian lunch of 120 people, the majority of people were White. [Laughter] We can't do it. I don't think God wants us to do it.

In addition to the Scriptures, the theological categories of the Reformed tradition lent weight to this commitment to multiculturalism. Particularly, the Reformed tradition's emphases on the covenant and the glory of God were an aid to this work.

SHELTON: If you are really committed to covenant theology and its implications, we will be pursuing this practically speaking . . . The reformers were not thinking racial and ethnic community, but read what . . . was written in the Scriptures about our being called to mutual love and esteem. It's already there, in what we say we believe and are committed to.

WB: Do you feel like Calvinism has the resources to help us through these things?

BRIAN: Absolutely. I think it's there in spite of the fact that we haven't opened it up, so we haven't embraced it fully to how it addresses the questions for minority abuse and systemic evil. But I think it's there. I think it has the potential. . . . We have got to get out of individualistic thinking and begin to think covenantally. You know, it's in our theology, but we don't think that way as a denomination yet. Our theology will lead us there, but we are not there yet. We still think it's individual hard work.

FERNANDO: True diversity is not assimilating minorities into majority culture. True diversity is being able to embrace those cultural differences that bring out the glory of God.

JIMMY: Not just for the sake of self-preservation but for the glory of God. . . . It's not diversity for the sake of having different colored faces, and saying, 'Now all of you politically correct liberal people can get off my back.' It's to the greater glory of God that we express the expansiveness of his love and of his kingdom vision. It's his greater glory.

A noteworthy exception in this discussion came from Marshall, who was outspoken on his perception that there needed to be Black PCA churches. At first, this puzzled me: Was he advocating for segregated churches? Was this coming from a purely pragmatic position, that because multiethnic churches did not work, they should not be attempted, in spite of theological commitments? However, upon reflection, I eventually landed on this conclusion: Marshall is committed to a truly diverse church, but he recognizes that multiethnicity does not automatically equal true diversity. He views diversity through the broader ecclesiological lens of denominations—i.e., congregations with a strong majority Black culture will create a truly multicultural denomination. I believe that in his mind, having Black PCA churches would actually help create a truly diverse PCA, rather than making the PCA only superficially diverse. If my interpretation is correct, Marshall simply holds to a highly nuanced view of culture and a commitment to diversity. His expression may differ from some of the more optimistic pastors, but the core goal remains the same: diversity within the PCA. A few quotations from my interview with him bear this out:

> The PCA is a culture; it's not just a people of particular beliefs. It's very much a culture. And so, as an African American, to come in to the PCA, you realize that you're walking into another culture.
>
> We don't plant Black PCA churches; we're into Blacks pastoring White Churches.
>
> [I say] y'all should be planting Black churches, and they get hostile. We plant *churches*. No, they don't; they plant *White* churches! You sort of ignore the obvious, because you ignore that you're a culture.
>
> I was for starting strong Black churches.
>
> I still think we need Black churches in the PCA if we're ever truly going to become a diverse denomination.
>
> See that's multicultural. You feel good about your [culture]. And let me feel good about mine. But that's difficult to do.
>
> They have the audacity to say this is something multicultural. It's multiethnic, not multicultural. Most of our churches are. They're multiethnic; they're not multicultural . . . there's nothing intrinsically wrong with that. My problem with the PCA is, don't try to make what is a multiethnic church a multicultural church

because that's not what it is. If it's multiethnic, that's fine. Just label it that.

Marshall's view has been forged through years of ministry in the PCA, many that included conflict, so he sees some of the darker sides of multicultural efforts. It may be harder for a White pastor or denomination to hear these words of challenge, yet his words provide an urgent call for majority pastors to listen up. It would be easier to dismiss him, because he is less positive about the realities of the PCA and very resistant to being forced to accommodate himself to the larger culture of the PCA. In his words: "Don't you think you could bend a little bit toward me? Why is it always me making myself palatable for you?" This perspective is valuable, since it cautions against church demographic triumphalism, which will only grind up more Black pastors as they are forced to assimilate into the majority culture.

FORMING LIFE-GIVING RELATIONSHIPS

In addition to a robust sense of call and foundational theological tenets, these pastors learn to thrive through community. First, these pastors find great strength and support through relationships with other minority pastors—in this community, the sense of outsiderness is shared among those who keenly feel the weight of the minority experience.

> THOMAS: I think that in terms of being an African American pastor in the PCA, it's really those connections with some of [the other Black pastors] that probably are the most life-giving. It keeps me going, keeps a perspective. They remind you that since you're doing it, then I could do it.
>
> MARTIN: At that point, there was already buy-in, I guess, to the church, and to people that you knew and then other African Americans... There was relational connection with White folks, but particularly with other African Americans, to say, 'Okay, we can kind of belong here together. And there's a reason that we've been drawn here.'
>
> MARTIN: I'm a part of a cohort with other [Black] pastors.
>
> FERNANDO: What I've learned is that I had to get to know the brothers and sisters who are stuck in this middle road, and realize that we are a culture within ourselves within the PCA. Connecting with them has helped me be able to persevere and realize that I don't have to deny who I am as a Black man to

fit; I can be who I am and it's okay. That has brought me great freedom. That has helped me to continue the journey.

MARSHALL: I have people that know me, know my struggles (implying other African American pastors).

In addition to providing day-to-day lifelines, these relationships also involve mentoring. Terrance, André, and Thomas all spoke to the role that older Black men played in their journeys:

TERRANCE: I just wondered, is there a place there for me or African Americans in general? And so, I just was hesitant. Then I got introduced to [a prominent Black scholar] and he connected me with this other guy [who was well connected in the PCA]. And I was able to meet him and talk with him, and then he got me connected with . . . a pretty diverse church.

ANDRÉ: But I've had especially two [Black] gentlemen that have just loved on me. One of them reached out to me when I was in seminary and basically kept saying, 'We need you in the PCA man. You've got to get ordained.' . . . So, he has been very instrumental, always checking in on me in terms of ministry, how things are going, and offering prayer. And the other gentleman is . . . near me, so we get to spend time every month, once every month . . . I was this close to quitting ministry, not to go on, and I was done, I was just done. And, yeah, he helped me keep my sanity.

THOMAS: [An older Black mentor in the PCA] was very helpful. He just kind of walked me through different steps. So those guys gave a more personal touch.

At the same time, these pastors also intentionally spoke of the value of multiethnic and cross-cultural friendships. As Marshall summarized, "I'm into people and relationships . . . And I have relationships with White ministers. If you don't have that, you're not truly multicultural. You're something else; again, you're code switching."

The value of these relationships, in addition to ordinary pastoral friendships, lies specifically in the additional shouldering of the burden of racial reconciliation. For several pastors, the friendship with White pastors was at its most fruitful when there was a sense of welcome, an attitude of open conversation, especially on matters of race, and the presence of advocacy and solidarity. According to Anthony, "I think things like this [interview] are helpful and important to know . . . that my voice would be heard and some of the things that I'm dealing with as a minister, as an African

American minister." The presbytery is one organic place for the formation of such relationships; as Terrance put it, "I love my presbytery. [They've] been very welcoming. Very kind. I've got a lot of friends. And guys like to talk openly about this stuff. And we do. And I've been highly encouraged to be involved." Of the pastors interviewed, Jimmy and Desmond spoke the most at-length about the need for such advocacy and solidarity. Jimmy related his experience of the 2016 Racial Reconciliation Overture.

> JIMMY: What mattered a lot to me is that there were people that I've known for some time now who were not allies when I first met them. They didn't care about the stuff when I first met them, but now they do. And now they are some of the most fronted voices. They are some of the first people to rise up and defend those who are being disenfranchised. They are the first to speak now, and to see that happening feels more like family. That feels more like the kind of warm-hearted Christianity that I imagine John 17 was all about in the first place. That is the kind of corporate witness that will create the union and communion for which we were made. When that happens, when I feel like I am on the Others' mind, and they speak up before I have a chance to speak up—because it is exhausting to be one of the [at that time] fifty-two African American Teaching Elders. Everyone is always saying, 'What do you think about this?' It is exhausting. I'm tired. But on the other hand, I realized the responsibility that I have to speak, and so I try to appreciate it, but it feels really good for other people to be speaking on it as well. This is not just for the benefit of Black folk. This is for the benefit of all of us.

Desmond spoke about the benefit of having openness in relationships.

> DESMOND: Now of course there are also the joys of seeing people who want authentic relationships and they don't want you to hide yourself. They do want you to share that. They want to enter into that. They want to say, 'If I'm going to know you and actually love you, I've got to know all of you and love all of you [Pastor]. You can't hide that part from me. I may not understand it all. I may need to learn a lot, but I'm willing to do that.' So that's really helpful. It's a joy to see people come together and sort of ache over the same things that you ache over, to have the same longings . . .

What is the fruit of such openness and shared longings?

> DESMOND: Those are some of the joys and some of the encouragements that you take when you know that you can meet with

people. And because you have talked about issues of race deeply, when you meet together again, you don't have to talk about issues of race. You can talk about any number of other things. And should the issue of race come up, I don't have to hide myself. I don't have to put up my shield like the Starship Enterprise. I don't have to do that. Because I'm not going to be immediately attacked if I bring up something connected to that. So as our conversation flows, it just flows naturally from topic to topic. And one of the topics that will come up sometimes is something having to do with race. Many times, within a Reformed context, depending on where you are, I can't even go there because it will be immediately judged as liberal, as unbiblical, as having nothing to do with the gospel, and therefore out of bounds immediately.

WB: I guess I'm hearing a theme of trust.

D: Yes.

When asked what White pastors could do to develop this type of trust, supporting Black pastors in their ministry, Desmond had the following advice:

> DESMOND: PCA pastors say to me, 'Well there's no way I can integrate my hometown because we're 99 percent White in a White community in my city.' But in a sense, I would say . . . [White pastors] can acknowledge my world from the pulpit . . . The other way is to acknowledge that the ground of what we're doing is biblical. I think that is so important to say, 'You know, what these brothers are doing is biblical.' . . . And then say, 'I'm willing to listen and not automatically judge and say this is out of bounds.'

Whereas minority relationships help reduce the feeling of isolation that comes from being an outsider, these cross-cultural friendships allow minority pastors to feel less like outsiders and more like co-laborers with valuable contributions, gifts, and vantage points. In Shelton's words,

> How much of a joy is it when our White brothers embrace the *de facto* privilege they have and want to put it to good use, in the sense of doing the heavy lifting of exposing to the congregations and others what that privilege is, and how to use it to embrace their brothers and sisters in Christ. When we see that happening, that's like wind to the sails. That is one of the ways to help with minority fatigue: keep it from getting overwhelming.

THINKING STRATEGICALLY ABOUT THE FUTURE

A third aspect of learning to thrive involves thinking strategically about the future by investing in the PCA for long-term future gains. This involves engaging the PCA in four ways. First, there is a concerted effort to network specifically within the Black community of pastors and congregants. Second, there is an increased focus on getting people of color to serve in denominational agencies and in key leadership positions. Third, there is a desire to see denominational resources directed toward the work of recruiting and sustaining Black ministers. At the same time, these men are pastors at heart. While there is a specific focus on the PCA as an institution, there remains a clear focus on pastoral ministry as a way of changing the culture. For these elders, the work of developing a graciously multiethnic denomination takes place primarily at the level of the individual's heart. Therefore, the fourth mode of strategic thinking is a commitment to the hard and humble work of local pastoral care.

Developing Networks for Minority Leaders

Many of these Black pastors see the need to develop organic relationships into formalized networks of Black leaders in ministry. While these networks have been in operation for many years, many of these pastors desire to invest in them for the sake of future African American PCA leaders. A stronger network of Black pastors helps sustain ministry through invigorating events and conferences. As Thomas recalls, the power of being around other Black brothers in worship can be tremendously encouraging: "I went to a convocation, an African American Reformed convocation out of [a Southern city] . . . I found that I could also not just be a kind of college-educated Gen-Xer, young professional type, but also I could be Black, because there were Black people there . . . it was all Black." The New City Network (a network of multiethnic church plants with regular gatherings and conferences), the PCA's African American Ministries Network, and the annual Leadership Development Resource (LDR) conference were the most frequently named networks, when asked what enabled these pastors to thrive and be supported in ministry.

A stronger network of Black pastors also provides a mechanism for newer pastors to find mentors, avoiding the more painful challenges of previous generations who struggled through their first years of ministry in relative isolation. Fernando spoke poignantly about this need:

> One of the things I'm passionate about now is being for other young African Americans what I didn't have . . . Every person that God put in my life loved me well, but I'd never had an African American Teaching Elder to truly sit under to help me navigate the PCA culture, PCA politics. Because no matter how much my majority-culture brothers love me, they are never going to be able to understand what it's like to be Black in the PCA. They can love me. They can sympathize with me, but they'll never be able to understand fully what it means to be in my shoes and in my world. But other African American TEs . . . can sympathize and understand. So, I want to give to the younger generation something I didn't have, and that is mentorship from an older African American TE who's been in the denomination for a long time. Most of the brothers and sisters that end up leaving, it's not over theology; it's over the cultural dynamics of dominant culture/subdominant culture stuff . . . Part of the reason why we [want to network] is to help those African American men and women who are struggling culturally with identity. Who am I? How can I be a Black man and plant in the PCA? . . . What does that look like? How do I get by? How do I make it when these things come up? They need to hear from older African Americans. This is what it's like. This is what we went through. You can get through, but you got to connect with us. If you don't connect with the other African Americans, it's going to be hard. You got to have relationships with the other brothers and sisters that are in the denomination.

One explicit difference between two pastors regarded the work of recruitment: Do these networks exist to recruit African Americans into the PCA while in seminary or from other denominations? While many spoke of this reality, and one pastor went so far as to say that he does recruit, Alexander's viewpoint emphasized how his relationship with the PCA was more organic than structural: "I can't say definitively that [explicit recruiting] is not happening and I'm not going to say that's not one method that should be sought after. My experience wasn't like that; it was very organic."

Institutional Focus (Agencies and Leadership)

In addition to these formalized networks, most pastors agreed that thinking strategically meant thinking about denominational structures and leadership. In Anthony's words, "I think there need to be more African Americans in seats of influence who understand the issues of race in terms of being an African American and what our communities go through." Lest this be thought of as mere power-grabbing, the interviewees viewed such leadership opportunities as chances to have their voices heard and have the majority culture grow in understanding.[3] Furthermore, others felt that this privilege ought to be extended beyond the Black community. Both Desmond and Terrance expressed the desire to see people from a multitude of ethnic backgrounds addressing the denomination through positions of leadership. This would further the work of reconciliation, because as Terrance insisted, "We need to hear different perspectives."

Of the TEs interviewed, Desmond had the most comprehensive list of institutional leadership possibilities:

> Some type of conference, workshop at General Assembly about cultural intelligence, trying to make it a priority to have minority TEs preach at General Assembly . . . Referring minority pastors to be on committees, directors of agencies, those are tangible things the denomination can do to show . . . we want to be diverse in a way that's healthy. Those would be some things that I'd recommend.

Institutional Focus (Resources and Equipping)

In addition to placing individuals into positions of leadership, thinking strategically about the future involves utilizing the denomination's resources. At least half of the pastors interviewed benefitted tremendously from denominational resources, from seminary scholarships for minorities, to funds for church planting and ministry development. Jimmy beautifully summarized this work: "They used their cultural and financial power and resources to be a blessing to us." Seminary scholarships loomed large in these pastors'

---

3. Alexander spoke strongly against the desire simply to have people in leadership to increase power. Instead, having minorities in positions of influence aids cultural growth: "That's why when we talk about things like having more representation of African Americans or minorities in positions within the PCA, most people think power: 'Oh we should give them more power, so they can do that.' Now. . . the power paradigm I think is poisonous. That's not what you're doing. . . If you add African Americans to your leadership on your church on your boards or whatever, they bring up, they add a particular type of culture that forces you to adopt that culture onto your base culture." At the same time, Alexander was skeptical that a top-down approach to multiculturalism would work to create long-term change: "If that doesn't happen at the grassroots level there is nothing that the 'PCA *qua* PCA,' as the leadership can ever do." Like many of the pastors interviewed, Alexander viewed the local congregation as the most powerful locus for denominational change. This will be addressed below.

minds when considering how to share resources. Thomas explained the importance of having financial resources for minority students to enter seminary:

> If God is calling some young Black men to ministry ... generally speaking, providentially speaking, they are going to have less money than your average White person. There's just going to be less funding, so you don't want money to be a hindrance, especially in a fairly affluent denomination like the PCA ... You want to make sure ... as much as possible, that you are financially present. That's a pretty straightforward [way to help].

This is especially important when finding ministers from inner-city contexts, such as Anthony's church:

> I don't think PCA has been very equipped to minister to, or support, or encourage ministers like myself, as an African American in this kind of context ... One of the things that we're very adamant about, where I am located, is raising up leaders from within our particular community. And we're in a predominantly African American community. The way the PCA is set up—in terms of ordaining ministers, and education, and things of that nature—doesn't always bode well when it comes to trying to identify who God is calling to ministry. And are we able to get them off to seminary, resources and things of that nature? The thing that's keeping them from moving forward is resources for education and ordination and things like that. So, you have a pool of people that you want to raise up and get them more involved in the PCA at an ordination-type level, but the things that they have to jump through in order to make it happen are quite a burden.

Though finances were the most frequently named beneficial resource, other interviewees also looked for educational resources. For example, André and Brian both expressed the desire to have the denomination invest more in publications by minorities on theological and cultural topics. Resources such as curricula, books, and other publications would be valuable aids for future minority leaders in the PCA.

Local Pastoral Focus

While institutional-level changes were a notable part of strategic thinking, the majority of comments concerned local pastoral ministry as the locus for investing in the future. This focus operated on two levels. First, these pastors felt the need to personally shape their churches to be spaces where other minorities felt comfortable. This often meant changing the worship service. As Alexander said, "I think it's up to individual churches, individual ministers, to make a concerted effort to allow what might be considered Black culture, or African American culture, or diverse culture to enter into the church." Such change is not always easy in a Presbyterian setting where the pastor has to work with other lay elders to make changes; in these settings, the pastor needs to first change the minds of these lay elders. André described this process with the leadership team at his church:

> I have to fight a battle with my session in terms of trying to show them that you can, in fact, remain biblically sound in terms of your worship service and be culturally relevant . . . [They say] 'You know, we invite Black people; they can come.' I'm like, 'Yeah, but come to what? When they come, where are they going to find their sense of identity? What is the one thing that's going to make them feel that they belong?'

For Terrance, allowing minorities to belong not only means having a blended worship service, but, just as importantly, allowing individuals to express themselves in their own cultural way: "Let people be who they are. Don't try to conform them into this Anglo way of looking at worship . . . That's not being the church, if we're trying to conform other people to look at it just the way I want them to look at it." One tangible way that these pastors attempt to influence the leadership culture at the church is through interns. As Terrance said, "I'm really big on getting interns . . . We need to keep having windows of opportunity given to people who are different."

As these pastors reflected on their commitment to local pastoral ministry, a second level of emphasis emerged: the simple ability of relationships to bring about change. Almost all believed that the most meaningful changes occur through relationships. Of course, each pastor went about it in different ways. Alexander declared that, unlike "some people [who] wear the fact that they are a minority on their sleeves, my philosophy has always been stealth, coming in, establishing a relationship. And through establishing relationships . . . they'll come to Jesus eventually." For Thomas, the emphasis on local relationships comes down to the logic of love: "I just think of the incarnation as very local. You can't love somebody from a distance. Love is concrete, love is tangible, doing what you do in person . . . in terms of tangible love, tangible things, local is where it's really meaningful." For Jimmy, love wedded with localism was the only way to prevent diversity from becoming legalistic:

The minute you begin to prescribe something, we just have the capacity to check the box and then think that the job is done. But it is really a matter of love at the end of the day. Isn't love the final apologetic? Isn't love the final arbiter of whether or how good a job we are doing at this? When people of color are voicing how loved they feel, when outsiders are expressing how loved they understand themselves to be in our place, in our denomination and churches, then I think we are making the [right] decisions. Those concrete things are a part of it, and they are important, and they are necessary, but I am more interested in the heart getting there.

Fernando echoed this sentiment. It is only through relationships that one can learn to see the world through the eyes of another:

> When there is no relationship with people, you look at social issues differently. If I have a relationship with someone, then issues of race and justice aren't just political issues . . . So, relationships are important when it comes to understanding; there's only so much you can get from a book, only so much you can get from a seminar, if you're not breaking bread with people, inviting people into your homes, sitting down talking with one another, doing life together, having genuine relationships.

In the gritty and slow work of pastoral relationships, these pastors are investing in the future of the PCA, making their congregations places where minorities are welcome and majority-culture Christians grow in Christlike hospitality and sacrifice. Through these local ministry settings, these pastors are developing resiliency and learning to thrive.

PRACTICING GRATITUDE

Practicing gratitude is the final way these pastors are learning to thrive in the PCA. Some interviewees were quite exuberant in their gratitude. Even in the interviews with those who have been badly wounded in the PCA, gratitude bleeds through. Part of their gratitude is simple realism. Each pastor has assessed his ministry in the PCA with sobriety and, upon looking at the other church options available, made the decision to, in Jimmy's words "bloom where you are planted." Jimmy simply recognized the inability to escape the racial tensions in the PCA by going somewhere else: "It would just be chasing the unicorn at some level, to try and find that magic place where I don't have to face racism, or I don't have to deal with disappointment. This is the evangelical church. It is the birthmark of evangelical Christianity. It is in the warp and woof; it's part of the air we breathe."

In addition to submitting to the reality that no church is perfect, these pastors choose to be grateful for the positive changes they see in the PCA. As Desmond put it, "Every denomination has flaws. The PCA has grown a great, great deal." According to Terrance, "I'm encouraged. It's not perfect, no, but we are making progress, significant progress." Or as Brian said, reflecting on two decades of ministry in the PCA, "I feel more supported now than I've ever felt." For André, witnessing the denominational efforts toward reconciliation were of great encouragement:

> I've had some great experiences within the PCA. One of them was the 2016 General Assembly with racial reconciliation issues at the GA. I mean, that was just a tremendous occasion, just watching this monumental thing happen. I know so many brothers and sisters, minority brothers and sisters, have been praying for this a long time, way before my time. And so to see them weeping and to see them just watch this happen before their very eyes was beautiful.

For Anthony, ministering in a poorer, inner-city church, being able to do the ministry he loves, gives him the encouragement he needs:

> The fact that I can be in the PCA and still be engaged in the type of ministry that I'm engaged in, having that freedom to do this is very, very important to me, which shows me that the PCA is not trying to be monolithic in their approach to church planting or what churches should look like. And granted, you do have those folks out there. But the fact that in a context where I'm afforded the freedom to be who I am as a minister to the church, to reflect the community that it's in, means a great deal to me.

Gratitude enabled Terrance to have compassion for those White ministers who might be slower to speak out on matters of race. In this quote, he beautifully models the compassionate ability to see the world through another's eyes:

> In fairness to my Anglo brothers specifically, at least [in the South] it takes great courage for them to really take a stand on these issues, and to be willing to talk of this in church, especially if they're established and around awhile . . . They've got people in churches who got money, got influence. You know this is scary for them. They could lose their job, lose the heart of their congregations. And I'm not letting them off the hook either. I'm just saying, like, c'mon, let's be honest. That would be really hard. I don't care what race you are. Culture and our ethnic tribes . . . those are powerful, powerful influences in our

lives. And especially for our Southern brothers . . . [For me] I might lose my church. They might lose families; they might lose relatives . . . I think I'm probably not going to give your typical African American perspective . . . I still think they need to make their stand for what's right. All I'm saying is, we also need to have some compassion too. . . There's a lot at stake for everybody. And they need to pay the cost, of course. But I'm just saying, man, let's have some compassion.

By recognizing God's hand in their lives and ministries, and by naming the signs of growth, these pastors grow in the resiliency needed to thrive. Even through the struggles, they have the opportunity to witness and participate in the changes God is bringing in the PCA. Alexander recounted the joy of having a front-row seat to appreciate God's redemptive work:

Back in the 1980s, the church that I'm currently at, there was a Black, truly African American, that came in. He was from Africa and he was an American. He came in the church. He and his wife sat down. He came several times. And an elder visited him and told him that he didn't think that this was the church for him, because him being there with his wife communicated something, a particular value, cultural value, that he felt. . . it wasn't what they wanted to teach their young people . . . Now this [man], he was actually a pastor, but he got his PhD in psychology, and he was a professor at this time, but he was also looking for a place to worship. So, he essentially stopped coming, because he was told that his continued presence was viewed as communicating something to the young people that was unhealthy. So, he left and started another church with the purpose of being more diverse. The church didn't succeed. So, anyway, many years later, back to 2015, he says, 'You know I need to worship somewhere. I'm going to give [name of church] another try. Because, you know, last time I was there, they told me I couldn't come, but surely things are different.' So, he walks in, and the day he walks in, I'm preaching. He flashed a big smile on his face. I finished preaching, and he made a beeline to me and just hugged me . . . he said he prayed. He was praying that the Lord would change the heart of the people there.

By savoring these glimpses of redemption, these minority pastors gain strength to continue the journey of ministry in the PCA.

8

Conclusions

"We must accept finite disappointment, but never lose infinite hope."[1]
—Dr. Martin Luther King Jr.

Our exploration of race, doctrine, and culture in the PCA began with a few questions and a conviction. First, do the PCA's fundamental doctrinal commitments necessitate racial inclusion? According to the Scriptures, the Great Commission, and the Reformed tradition, the answer is yes. This leads to the second question: How well is that inclusion taking place? When we listen to the lived experiences of Black pastors in the PCA, we hear a story that is both sobering and encouraging: though welcomed inside the denomination, these pastors show the signs of racial fatigue brought about by being cultural outsiders. But instead of giving into exhaustion, these pastors developed resilience by learning to thrive in uncomfortable circumstances. We can answer the second question at least tentatively: inclusion is taking place, but not without struggle and pain. As much as the PCA has grown in racial reconciliation and inclusion since its inception, much more needs to be done. These realities gesture toward the conviction driving this research: the work of racial reconciliation is both necessary and possible.

---

1. King, *Words of Martin Luther King, Jr.*, 25.

CONCLUSIONS

A NECESSARY CONVERSATION

It should be no surprise that there is racial conflict within any denomination in the United States. The sheer volume of literature and personal witness dealing with race reveals how far racial division reaches, and these interviews are no different. As a culture, the PCA exhibits troubling signs of exclusion, even while holding to convictions and desires that laud inclusion. This gap between theology and culture, between doctrine and practice, demands inspection. The work of racial reconciliation is necessary.

The importance of this conversation grows when we compare these stories with similar research in secular fields. Researchers studying the health of minorities working in majority-culture spaces have noted many ill effects that come from the extra stress of racial tension, labeling this complex of symptoms "racial battle fatigue." Racial battle fatigue describes "the physiological, psychological, and behavioral strain exacted upon racially marginalized and stigmatized groups. These excessive strains require additional energy redirected from more positive life fulfilling desires for coping with and fighting against mundane racism."[2] This is not mere academic jargon. There is a real-world cost to this fatigue, including

> increased levels of psychosocial stressors and subsequent psychological (e.g., frustration, shock, anger, disappointment, resentment, hopelessness), physiological (e.g., headache, backache, "butterflies," teeth grinding, high blood pressure, insomnia), and behavioral responses (e.g., stereotype threat, John Henryism, social withdrawal, self-doubt, and a dramatic change in diet).[3]

For majority-culture Christians with minority leadership, such a list ought to solicit compassion and curiosity: Does my church culture cause my

---

2. Smith et al., "Racial Battle Fatigue," 66. A few words about racial battle fatigue: As an academic interpretive hermeneutic, it is grounded in Critical Race Theory (CRT), which is a lightning rod for evangelical controversy. Yet, as simple descriptive language, racial battle fatigue reveals a common experience without demanding adherence to the central presuppositions of CRT. For example, when discussing this with numerous Black PCA leaders, I simply said "I'm reading about something called 'racial battle fatigue,'" and the ubiquitous response was, "Yes, that describes it well." Even without prior exposure to the concept, these leaders intuitively sensed the truth to the label "racial battle fatigue": they were fatigued and embattled because of their race in a less-than-hospitable culture, as the interviews bear out. It would be inappropriate to dismiss these interviews, or label them as coming from a "liberal" or "progressive" agenda. The interviews speak for themselves. The additional lens of racial battle fatigue simply offers an interdisciplinary dialogue partner to further our analysis.

3. Smith et al., "Racial Battle Fatigue," 68.

pastor debilitating health problems? Does my pastor experience harm in our community?

There is a haunting symmetry when comparing church cultures with the secular cultures considered in racial battle fatigue studies.[4] First, Black PCA pastors experience cultural dissonance, alongside their counterparts in secular spaces. According to one study, minority professors recorded a sense of "being out of place" in primarily White spaces: "Black faculty can experience aspects of racial battle fatigue by feeling isolated, feared, unheard, outnumbered, and feeling an out-of-place-ness."[5] According to the interviews, one could easily substitute "Black pastors" for "Black faculty" and achieve an identical sentiment.

Second, Black pastors endure exclusionary behavior as minorities in a White context, even if it is implicit or unintended. At first glance, one might be tempted to dismiss an unknowing insult in the name of Christian charity; after all, maybe they didn't mean it, or didn't know any better. Yet, the desire to protect a congregant from the possibility of shame must not trump the need for church leaders to minimize exclusionary behavior, however unintended. These negative interactions take a toll:

> While people of color may feel insulted, they are often uncertain why, and perpetrators are unaware that anything has happened and are not aware they have been offensive. For people of color, they are caught in a Catch-22. If they question the perpetrator . . . denials are likely to follow. Indeed, they may be labeled "oversensitive" or even "paranoid." If they choose not to confront perpetrators, the turmoil stews and percolates in the psyche of the person, taking a huge emotional toll. In other words, they are damned if they do and damned if they don't.[6]

As shown earlier, numerous pastors experience this internal struggle. Though their testimonies suggest such interactions are not daily events in their lives, the emotional cost still accumulates over time. Church leadership must be aware of such long-term detrimental effects and work to foster inclusive cultures, where exclusionary comments are discussed in a context of grace, so that apology can be extended, forgiveness granted, and community restored.

    4. The literature on racial battle fatigue is extensive. For the purposes of this report, two studies are considered: one reporting on Black faculty and one reporting on the campus experiences of Latino/a students. Though these groups are not identical, there are important experiential overlaps that make for a meaningful comparison with this study on Black PCA pastors.

    5. Arnold et al., "Psychological Heuristics and Faculty of Color," 903.

    6. Sue, "Racial Microaggressions in Everyday Life," para. 19.

Third, Black pastors need gatherings where they are not the minority. Research on the habits of minority students show the benefits of "social counterspaces," or gatherings of students of the same ethnicity, where minorities become the majority.[7] These counterspaces offer students an opportunity to rest and refresh from the burden of being a minority. In fact, these "students' resilience depend on their ability to draw on the cultural knowledge, skills, and contacts from their home communities" in these social counterspaces.[8] All of the Black pastors similarly noted the benefit of social counterspaces.[9] Unfortunately, Whites often misunderstand such counterspaces, calling them exclusionary or even racist.[10] Due to the possibility of misunderstanding, White Christians should listen to the research. Social counterspaces foster resilience. For these pastors, some time spent in a monocultural space as a majority refreshes them for being a minority in the multicultural space of the PCA. Church leaders should encourage the formation of ministries that allow minorities space to be in the majority. This is a practical investment in ministry longevity and a worthy expression of solidarity and love.

Finally, even signs of resilience must be considered against the backdrop of racialized fatigue. As studies of minority faculty show, in an effort to retain personal dignity, these faculty attempt to "maintain agency by identifying and choosing [a] personal locus [of control]," using adversity to generate an internal sense of power or self-ownership.[11] This decision creates an impression of resilience but can also cause deeper problems. The choice to overcome adversity requires a constant expenditure of energy that drains resources over the long haul.[12] For Black pastors, the effort to thrive

---

7. Yosso et al., "Critical Race Theory," 677.

8. Yosso et al., "Critical Race Theory," 677.

9. One significant example of this is the LDR conference, which fosters a sense of community among Black Presbyterians. LDR was regarded highly by many of the pastors interviewed; as Martin said, "the LDR conference is the best conference of the year."

10. Yosso et al., "Critical Race Theory," 677. Similarly, LDR has faced backlash from those who question the emphasis on creating a racially monocultured space (see, e.g., Wilson, "Conservative Presbyterian Seminary in St. Louis").

11. Arnold et al., "Psychological Heuristics and Faculty of Color," 911.

12. Hence the phenomenon of "John Henryism": a coping strategy that focuses on high effort and achievement to improve social standing. As implied by the name, the success that comes from this hard work comes with a high price. For instance, one study exploring the impact of John Henryism on the mental health of African Americans found it linked with higher levels of depression: "When faced with unfair treatment and other stressors, African Americans who use high-effort coping could negatively affect their mental health . . . The observed relationship between John Henryism and depression in this study suggests that engaging in high-effort coping is associated with greater likelihood of depression among African Americans." Church leaders must be

often looks like increased commitment to the PCA, a sort of doubling down in the denomination. While this is a positive reaction in the face of conflict, church leadership must not receive increased commitment naively. For some, increased commitment to the PCA might constitute a coping mechanism to handle the stress of being a minority. As the research indicates, even positive coping mechanisms are costly.

This is a necessary conversation, indeed. Any gap between the Scripture's ethical mandates and an institution's practices calls for sanctification, especially when that gap mirrors the practices of the secular cultures surrounding the church. Christians are called to "put off your old self, which belongs to your former manner of life and is corrupt through deceitful desires," and "put on the new self, created after the likeness of God in true righteousness and holiness" (Eph 4:22–24). Calling for racial reconciliation in the PCA is simply part of pastoral work, encouraging the denomination to "make every effort to supplement your faith with virtue, and virtue with knowledge, and knowledge with self-control, and self-control with steadfastness, and steadfastness with godliness, and godliness with brotherly affection, and brotherly affection with love" (2 Pet 1:5–7). The church's holiness demands this conversation.

So do Christian love and hospitality. As 2 Peter 1 indicates, sanctification leads to love. Christians must "welcome one another as Christ has welcomed you" (Rom 15:7). Christian fellowship requires solidarity with the suffering: "weep with those who weep" (Rom 12:15); "remember . . . those who are mistreated, since you are also one body" (Heb 13:3). Whenever a Christian laments of exclusion, the immediate response should not be scrutiny and suspicion, but love and welcome.

---

sensitive to such "high effort" coping mechanisms. After listening to the stories of the Black pastors in this study, one can easily imagine a freshly minted seminary graduate coming into a less-than-supportive church and seeking to overcome racial hostility by overworking, serving on multiple committees, and taking on unfair proportions of pastoral care or teaching or service-related work. In the end, this high-effort striving does not create mutuality and understanding, but simply mollifies the racial animus in the church culture, at extreme costs to the Black TE. The study hypothesized that a better way to handle stress was to have support from others, rather than to overcome stress through higher efforts of work: "It is possible that social support provided individuals with the resources necessary to cope with stress and minimizes the use of high-effort coping strategies." If so, Black pastors would benefit from their social support networks, like having a cohort of other Black pastors as a place to share painful stories, receive encouragement, and strategize for ways of preserving health. Hudson et al., "Racial Discrimination, John Henryism," 235–36.

Finally, ministerial health requires this conversation. If the PCA's Black pastors exhibit signs of racialized fatigue, there is great cause for concern.[13] The New Testament is clear: the church must care for her ministers:

> Let the elders who rule well be considered worthy of double honor, especially those who labor in preaching and teaching. For the Scripture says . . . 'the laborer deserves his wages.' (1 Tim 5:17–18)

> We ask you, brothers, to respect those who labor among you and are over you in the Lord and admonish you, and to esteem them very highly in love because of their work. (1 Thess 5:12–13)

> One who is taught the word must share all good things with the one who teaches. (Gal 6:6)

Presbyterian churches vow to support their pastors. In addition to providing adequate payment to "free [ministers] from worldly cares and avocations," churches promise to give their pastors "all proper support, encouragement, and obedience in the Lord."[14] When a pastor's ministerial health is compromised, the church must be concerned. And when numerous minority pastors humbly express a shared testimony of marginalization, the church must work to change. Racial reconciliation is necessary.

A POSSIBLE CONVERSATION

At the same time, Christians cannot lose hope. The work of racial reconciliation is not only necessary, but also possible. The Scriptures and church tradition contain all the necessary tools for such a work. A wide array of theological concepts enable Christians to engage in racial reconciliation, such as the dignity and purpose of creation, the shared image of God, the impact of sin, the scope of redemption, the possibility of repentance, and the assurance that the triune God is invested in transformation. This study, furthermore, has shown an additional resource: the diverse church community. Minority Christians are not passive recipients of reconciliation; they

---

13. Because of this, it is imperative for minority pastors to practice self-care. As discussed above, research into racial battle fatigue and other race-related conditions reveals increased risk to both physical and mental health when working in racially hostile cultures. Minority pastors must heed these warnings and take extra precautions to protect their physical and emotional well-being. Successful coping strategies may include an increased focus on physical fitness, mental health counseling, and participation in systems of support, such as the social counterspaces where they are in the majority. Having healthy Black pastors is a ministerial necessity for churches.

14. Presbyterian Church in America, *Book of Church Order*, 20.6.

are co-laborers in it. Their testimonies valuably point out blind spots within the majority culture and offer resources for redemptive relationships. At the same time, as their stories attest, minority pastors are often pegged as the sole resource for racial understanding. This causes them to spend copious amounts of time having the same conversations over and over, sapping their reserves and limiting their impact in other church matters.[15] Clearly, mutuality is called for. Together in Christ and working through the power of the Spirit, the work of reconciliation is possible.

So, what can Christians and church leaders do to promote reconciliation?[16] If we are led by the voices in this study, the primary challenge facing many minority Christians is a culture of exclusion within the majority culture. This culture of exclusion is at odds with the biblical narrative and Reformed theology. Thus, to move forward in racial reconciliation via increased inclusion, two things are needed. Together, Christians of all races must identify cultures that wound. Then, together, they must cultivate cultures that heal—communities marked by cultural intelligence, fellowship, and intimacy.

Identify Cultures That Wound

As Marshall stated in his interview, "The PCA is a culture . . . not just a people of particular beliefs. It's very much a culture." While most White PCA leaders may consider the PCA to be simply a doctrinal organization, from the vantage point of these minority pastors, the PCA is a distinct culture. As evidenced in these interviews, one aspect of the PCA's culture is what Korean American pastor Duke Kwon terms "White Cultural Normativity."[17]

---

15. As Jimmy lamented earlier, "I have been deemed by the [Local] Presbytery as capable of speaking to the whole counsel of God, not just the issue of race."

16. In asking the question this way, I am trying to incorporate the insights from several of my interviewees regarding the church as institution. Specifically, their emphasis on localism discourages me from asking "What can the church learn?," as if denominations were a monolithic entity, rather than a collection of disparate networks, congregations, leaders, and relationships.

17. Kwon, "Denominational Diversity and Cultural Normativity." Admittedly, this type of language is often off-putting to a culture that does not usually think reflectively about its existence as a culture. The dominant culture often struggles to understand what a culture is. According to Carl Ellis, "culture embodies the cumulative effect of history, destiny, and consciousness in the life of a people" (Ellis, *Free at Last?*, 26). J. Kameron Carter offers this picture of culture apart from race: "culture as marked by '"the genius" of "a people,"' while at the same time not rooting genius in biology, causes other factors, such as the social and historical determinations of culture(s) to figure centrally" (Carter, *Race*, 131). Admittedly, this is a fine line to walk. Some may cry foul at the

This normativity shows up in the subtle suggestions that the White cultural way of doing ministry is somehow better or more acceptable than other cultural expressions. "White Cultural Normativity" often masquerades as simple personal preference, but in fact perpetuates racial inhospitality and exclusion when it becomes entrenched in a system, lauded and taught as the right way to minister or worship.[18]

White Cultural Normativity thrives in settings where culture is ignored or assumed to be neutral. This is what makes such normativity so insidious within the church. Under the guise of inclusivity, Christians create boundaries that isolate and wound other Christians. Until majority-culture Christians and leaders recognize that their church or denomination possesses a distinctive culture, there will be no impetus to pursue cultural intelligence, which would enable them to navigate cultural difference and move toward hospitality. When a dominant culture operates without cultural intelligence, there is a much higher chance that minority pastors and congregants will experience racial burnout. Worse still is the reality that when these minority brothers and sisters experience burnout, they will be blamed for it, because the majority culture will not recognize its own contribution to the problem. If minority pastors leave the ministry due to racialized fatigue, the perception will be that they were not strong enough for ministry. If minority members leave culturally White churches (even if the churches are multiethnic, following Marshall's insights), they will be labeled divisive or fragile.

Sadly, doctrinal confession alone does not prevent a Christian organization from wounding its members. A culture that wounds may say "all races welcome," yet mean, "all races welcome *on our terms*," or "all races welcome, but *not all cultures* welcome." A culture that wounds may hold the Bible central to life and ministry and prize the gospel above all else, yet fail to recognize the ethical demands of God's word for human relationships. A culture that wounds may confess the communion of the saints, yet defend

---

supposition that one can speak about "a people" at all without being in some way racist. But, by decentering the ontology of race, experience can be allowed to come forward, allowing nuance and variegation within groups sharing a similar history. Indeed, this is the way that many minority individuals speak about their experiences—as having both a corporate and individual dynamic.

18. Similarly, Christians must be thoughtful when discussing personal preferences. In Christ, there is freedom of conscience, and on the surface personal preferences contribute to the church's diverse witness. However, we must hold our preferences with gentleness and discernment. Personal tastes are usually wedded to larger stories of family history and cultural location. The work of reconciliation will entail the harder work of introspection, holding one's own preferences up for critique and allowing for the likelihood that, instead of simple neutral goods, our personal preferences are also products of a beautiful, but broken world. We should celebrate all things good, while also acknowledging the impact of sin on our personal preferences and cultural expressions.

those who exclude rather than those who are excluded. All Christians—whether White or minority, leadership or laity—must exercise discernment, listen to criticism, and ask probing questions. Through the fellowship of believers and the sanctifying critique of Scripture (2 Tim 3:16–17; Heb 4:12–13), it is possible to identify cultures that wound. And then, through the power of the Spirit of Christ, it is possible to cultivate the opposite: a culture that heals.

Cultivate Cultures That Heal

When Black pastors feel like outsiders in the PCA, it is primarily due to cultural differences. They long for true diversity, not mere tokenism or the pressure to conform. Many White church leaders want the same, but as Fernando said, "They have good intentions, but they lack the know-how; they lack the cultural intelligence." Cultural intelligence equips White Christians to embrace cultural diversity, instead of making cultural conformity a prerequisite for full inclusion.[19] It is one of the first steps toward embrace and intimacy, allowing minority Christians to enjoy full *racial* acceptance. With the history of racism in the United States, Black Christians have been denied full racial acceptance for generations, even within the church. As these ministers confessed, there is tremendous grief and frustration when one is unable to bring one's full self into ministry. Healing comes when one is accepted and welcomed. A culture that heals will be marked by racial hospitality, saying to minority Christians, "Bring your whole self into this ministry. You are welcome here."

There is a biblical and theological rationale for developing an inclusive culture that heals division. From the Reformed tradition, G. C. Berkouwer identifies the motivation for such a healing culture: our fellowship in Christ. Sensing that the intimate connection between Christ and his church forms an intimate connection between believers, Berkouwer says that union with Christ is "understood in the outlook on the earthly reality of the church . . . Fellowship arises here among those in whose midst he dwells and is present, fellowship in unity and concord, in knowledge, faith, and love. His nearness excludes 'schism' in the body."[20] The church belongs to Christ, and as such, believers belong to each other.

Mutual belonging brings healing. In Christ, skin color and culture are decentered as the locus of identity and belonging, but they are not removed.

---

19. For an excellent resource on cultural intelligence, see Livermore, *Cultural Intelligence*.

20. Berkouwer, *Church*, 90.

Instead, they are allowed to flourish as marks of grace. Through the work of the Spirit, these areas of difference become opportunities for service, ornaments in the church, and instruments for God's glory. Previously, "culture [was] the site of closure and containment," but with eyes looking for Christian diversity and hearts longing for Christian unity, there is now the opportunity for "cultural intimacy and thus reciprocity."[21] When believers belong mutually to each other, cultural exchange and expansion become the norm, and a redeemed appreciation for cultural diversity arises. As Willie James Jennings states, Christian "identity . . . draws definition from our cultural realities yet is determined by a new reality of love and belonging."[22] A new experience arises from the shared identity of Christian faith, where cultural distinctives are welcomed, not judged.

This transformation opens the door to intimacy. Because I can assume a shared foundation of identity in Christ, I am driven to become curious about the experience of others in the Christian family: What is the actual experience of persons of color within our church? Miroslav Volf calls this inquiry "double vision."[23] Once I have decided to move toward another in relationship, I must learn about this person. Double vision is the attempt to see the world "from here" (my perspective, which I do naturally) and "from there" (your perspective, which I am inclined to ignore unless I desire communion with you).[24] Such double vision is simply the horizontal, person-to-person dimension of Christian sanctification: "as we fix our eyes on Jesus, and focus on his kingdom, he doesn't blind our eyes toward our fellow believers; rather, he gives us new ways to consider them."[25] Once our eyes open, our hearts open too. The racial experiences of other Christians no longer seem like threats to my own cultural comfort, or opportunities to correct or instruct. Instead, the honest testimony of racial tension begins to drive a desire to grow and work toward mutual flourishing. This journey toward double vision can start with something as simple as a cup of coffee and a question posed: "So, what's it like to be Black in the PCA?"

Cultures that heal prioritize relationships. They do not seek the reconciliation of some theoretical "Other," but rather pursue intimacy with actual, in-the-flesh humans. Each healing culture will look and feel different depending on location and history, but there will be a similar spiritual integrity in each, as Christians eagerly move toward each other in mutual

---

21. Carter, *Race*, 230.
22. Jennings, *Christian Imagination*, 292.
23. Volf, *Exclusion & Embrace*, 216.
24. Volf, *Exclusion & Embrace*, 250–51.
25. Kruger, "Looking Over the Fence," para. 2.

belonging, "eager to maintain the unity of the Spirit in the bond of peace" (Eph 4:3).²⁶

This is an example of the type of localized reflection that leads to redemptive double vision. As White PCA leaders listen to the experiences of Black pastors, they will realize that their comfort in the denomination stems in part from their comfort in White racialized spaces. For people of color, race is an ever-present reality, while for most White, majority-culture people, it is a confusing, rarely acknowledged idea.²⁷ For those who instinctively dismiss the idea of racialized space as a thing of the past, Jennings offers a helpful analogy of architecture to describe the enduring effects of generations of racism: "Any house can be filled with new people and new practices, but the very shape of the house and where things are positioned exert a deep and abiding influence on those who live in the house."²⁸ PCA leaders must see that the "shape of the house" has been created, not just by the pursuit of doctrinal orthodoxy, but—as shown in chapter 1—by specific cultural preferences.

Second, after pondering this architectural metaphor, majority-culture PCA leaders will realize that the White racialized space of the PCA tends to be inhospitable to diverse cultural expressions. This forces minorities to experience the racial "double consciousness" mentioned earlier: the "peculiar sensation . . . of always looking at one's self through the eyes of others, of measuring one's soul by the tape of a world that looks on in amused contempt and pity. One ever feels his two-ness,—an American, a Negro; two souls, two thoughts, two unreconciled strivings, two warring ideals in one

---

26. This accords with a limitation inherent in phenomenology: the distinction between generalizability and transferability (see Auerbach and Silverstein, *Qualitative Data*, 86–87). Because generalizability is not the goal, this project is not a "PCA State of the Union," offering a full-scale evaluation of racial reconciliation in the denomination. Rather, the objectives are humbler: by faithfully describing the lived experience of one subgroup, crucial information can be gained to make a theory, which can be transferred to other subgroups with further inquiry. Opportunities abound to extend this research into other minority groups and cultures. For instance: Do Latino pastors feel the same pressure to conform as these Black pastors? What about Korean American pastors? Are these dynamics the same in other denominations, congregations, or neighborhoods? If denominations pursued systematic studies of their congregations and racial subgroups, they could gain a much deeper appreciation for the lived experiences of other "outsiders" inside the denomination. With each interview, the denomination could grow in empathy and seek to further tear down the cultural boundaries still present in the denomination. On a personal level, if every reader of this book began asking similar questions in their sphere of influence, indigenous cultures of healing would proliferate.

27. Hart, *Trouble I've Seen*, 48–49.

28. Jennings, *Christian Imagination*, 243.

dark body."[29] This "double consciousness" creates the racial fatigue described by these Black pastors, codified by researchers as racial battle fatigue.[30] As personal friends attest, "being Black in America is exhausting." Though they might not share many of these experiences, White PCA leaders need to heed these voices. Even if the conversation unearths disagreement, it still moves the community toward hospitality, as believers commit to the process of double vision, seeing the world through the eyes of another, because sanctification requires racial inclusion, even racial intimacy.[31]

Finally, the feedback of the double vision process will lead to a reevaluation of history. The majority culture's approach to history tends to assume neutrality. Minority voices often disagree. Rather than being neutral, "history does the work of identity formation."[32] In reading the history of the PCA, majority-culture leaders, in dialogue with their brothers and sisters of color, may discover that the popular narrative has rendered certain people invisible, or ignored important features of others' experiences.[33] Because history and identity reinforce each other, recovering forgotten heroes and discovering new ways of telling history that bring dignity and agency to minorities fosters a culture of intimacy, because "in order to foster a Christian imagination, we don't need to invent; we need to remember."[34] With an openness to learning through listening, church leaders can grow in the cultural intelligence necessary to cultivate cultures that heal.

TOWARD KOINONIA: "ALL RACES WELCOME, REALLY."

Studies on race often carry a hint of loneliness and isolation, of loss and absence. The weariness of the Black pastors I interviewed suggests an emptiness, the shadow of something missing. Echoing Berkouwer, the missing piece haunting conversations on race is fellowship, or *koinonia*. Conversations about *how* to understand race only scratch the surface of the deeper

---

29. du Bois, *Souls of Black Folk*, 2.
30. Smith et al., "Between Hope and Racial Battle Fatigue."
31. Volf, *Exclusion & Embrace*, 219, 252.
32. Carter, *Race*, 145.
33. Jennings, *Christian Imagination*, 114; Carter, *Race*, 145. An essential example of this recovery of hidden history is Equal Justice Initiative's memorialization of lynching in America. The silence of history regarding lynching leaves a lasting impact, one that EJI hopes to heal through acts of memorial. Equal Justice Initiative, *Lynching in America*.
34. Smith, *You Are What You Love*, 181.

spiritual need for *koinonia*: we were not created merely to understand, but to belong.

The Scriptures offer a powerful portrait of reconciliation, centered on this search for fellowship. For Christians seeking to push beyond mere understanding toward true intimacy, where outsiders become true insiders in cultures of healing, Paul's letter to Philemon offers a glimpse at what comes next. This letter holds promise for the PCA as a vision of "*koinonia*, Christian fellowship and mutual partnership." It is not simply a theological treatise about reconciliation, but "[it] is at a far deeper level an outworking . . . of that principle. That which it expounds, it also exemplifies."[35]

N. T. Wright views "the reconciliation of Philemon and Onesimus [as] an acted parable of the Gospel itself."[36] Any reading of Philemon must be understood against the backdrop of Paul's theology of reconciliation. Paul maintains that the confession "Jesus is Lord" concretely reorders the world of social strata. It removes any humanly erected borders and boundaries between Christians in the church, rendering no outsiders within the people of God.[37] After that fundamental reorientation, the work of the church is to actually live out this new reality through the power of the gospel, resulting in true *koinonia*, the "interchange and reciprocation of siblings."[38] As relationships become recalibrated around Christ, disparate individuals become a Christian family.

This recalibration is on display in Paul's letter to Philemon. First, Onesimus, the slave, is to be viewed as a brother in the Lord, a member of the family. This opens new possibilities for one formerly on the outskirts of society: "a place to stand, a status with some recognition, a family to call [his] own, a siblingship in a household, a task that was ennobling."[39]

Second, Philemon, the master, is called to embrace the returning brother, relinquishing the worldly aspiration of exacting justice in favor of extending grace.[40] This would be costly, especially to Philemon's pride, and so Paul reminds Philemon that Onesimus is not the only debtor. Onesimus is indebted to Philemon, but Philemon is indebted to Paul.[41] Philemon must

---

35. Wright, *Colossians and Philemon*, 175.

36. Wright, *Colossians and Philemon*, 174.

37. Gal 3:27–29; 1 Cor 1:22–25; Eph 2:11–22. Colossians 3:11 is especially important, since many scholars believe Paul's letter to Philemon was delivered along with the letter to the entire Colossian church (McKnight, *Letter to Philemon*, 3–4; see Wright, *Paul and the Faithfulness of God*, 1:33).

38. McKnight, *Letter to Philemon*, 71.

39. McKnight, *Letter to Philemon*, 26.

40. McKnight, *Letter to Philemon*, 98–103.

41. Phlm 19–20.

see himself and his entire household in relationship to Christ, with humble gratitude that drives mutual embrace.[42]

It could end there, with Philemon put in his place by the superior Paul, but Paul refuses to exempt himself from the recalibration of relationships through the gospel. Paul, the one with the greatest spiritual authority, becomes indebted to Philemon: "if he . . . owes you anything, charge that to my account . . . I will repay it."[43] He also lowers himself to a similar social status as Onesimus, reminding the church that he, Paul, was a prisoner dependent upon grace.[44] Like Onesimus, Paul is at the mercy of Philemon: it is only through the prayers of the saints that he has hope for deliverance.[45]

The goal of Paul's letter is *koinonia*, a reciprocal relationship of restoration and gratitude. As Philemon embraced his identity as a fellow debtor to Christ, he would welcome Onesimus as a brother, allowing the gospel to overturn the social strata of the Roman empire. Similarly, the apostle becomes a debtor, and begs for the intervention of the saints, hoping to be restored from prison through their prayers, so that the entire church reflects the new creation in Christ: "a new kind of society, a fellowship of equals in which the slave owner and slave were brothers (and sisters) in Christ."[46]

This "acted parable" demonstrates the gospel in action: outsiders become insiders through mutual embrace, as human-made boundaries are torn down through the ministry of Christ.[47] Such reconciliation is costly. Members must relinquish social power and cultural preference. But if Jesus is truly Lord of his church, the cost must be paid.[48] For White PCA leaders, racial inclusion and intimacy come with the price tag of humility. We are called to give up the comfort of exclusivity within cultures of White normativity that wound others by refusing them full racial status. We are simultaneously called to embrace diversity by cultivating cultures of intimacy, reciprocity, and welcome. If this seems too costly, consider the other parties involved:

---

42. Wright, *Paul and the Faithfulness of God*, 1:32.

43. Phlm 18–19.

44. Phlm 1, 9, 10, 13, 23. For this inversion of status, from apostle to prisoner, see McKnight, *Letter to Philemon*, 51–52.

45. Phlm 22. "Paul, like Onesimus, is in need of the powerful's decision on his behalf. Paul is laying before Philemon the opportunity to liberate a brother in Christ" (McKnight, *Letter to Philemon*, 110).

46. McKnight, *Letter to Philemon*, 5.

47. As such, it has incredible relevance for the modern church. As Scot McKnight passionately writes, this "demands our immediate attention: *the church is to be [the] first space of reconciliation in our communities, first among its own people and second as reconciled people who strive for reconciliation in society*" (McKnight, *Letter to Philemon*, 5, emphasis original).

48. Wright, *Colossians and Philemon*, 30.

for pastors of color, the cost of *koinonia* is far greater—leaving cultures of comfort, historical relationships, and ministry opportunities, and making a new home in an uncomfortable ecclesial space, all to pursue a vision of God's multiethnic church. *Koinonia* is costly for all Christians, but the sacrifice is worthwhile. It enables the church to look more like that envisioned in the Scriptures and church tradition: a communion of saints. Such fellowship is necessary, and it is possible through the redemptive work of God.

For the PCA, the ideals extolled in our founding documents demand a commitment to racial inclusion. For Christians of other traditions, the Scriptures and church history point to the same. By cultivating a culture of racial hospitality, the church can indeed become a place where all races are truly welcome, a place where the *shalom* of God rests in abundance. By welcoming racial outsiders to become insiders, the PCA will more fully be "faithful to the Scriptures, true to the Reformed faith, and obedient to the Great Commission."

Acknowledgments

It has been a privilege to work with an incredible array of pastors and theologians over the past several years throughout the formation of this project. Without the help and support of colleagues, family, and friends, it would have never made it this far. First and foremost, I would like to thank the twelve pastors interviewed in this project. Your trust, generosity, faith in Christ, and commitment to his church have been a continual inspiration. Thank you for your courage and your ministry. I am privileged to call you friends, mentors, fathers, and brothers, and it is an honor to dedicate this project to you.

To my dissertation advisor, Dr. Wesley Hill, you embody the ethic of friendship that is a constant theme in your scholarly work. Your gracious and incisive intellect continue to inspire. Thank you for your passion for justice and community, for making room for me to explore these important ideals, and for championing this project from the beginning. And to Dr. Carl Ellis, your participation in this project has been invaluable. Your scholarship has left an indelible mark on my thinking about gospel faithfulness and cultural discernment. Thank you for your steadfastness in this denomination. You are a hero in the faith and a mentor to me in ministry.

To the leadership and congregation of Christ Church of Arlington. I could have never completed this study without your support and enthusiasm. You have stood by me in many hard seasons and given me space to work on this manuscript in the midst of ministry. It has been a joy to serve here, and I pray that our small community can continue to show forth the glory of God's global church. Thank you for your love and encouragement.

A book never reaches this stage without much input from others. Shaun Cross, you are a true friend and brother, graciously giving me space to process ideas and make mistakes, and encouraging me from day one, when this project was an idea on a napkin. KJ Drake, Samuel Hall, Alex Ford, and Cyril Chavis, your thoughtful comments and interactions improved my writing and thinking immensely. Thank you all for your contributions to this book.

I extend the deepest thanks to my family: my children Sam, Luke, Jerem, and Eden, and especially my wife, Melynda. Thank you for putting up with the late nights of typing, for listening to my ruminations as I wandered the kitchen before dinners, and for allowing me time away to read, think, and write. I could not have done this without you, and it is my greatest honor to cultivate with you a household that experiences *shalom* and *koinonia*.

Finally, to the One who gives access to the Tree of Life for the healing of the nations, be honor, glory, and praise in the church, both now and forever.

Bibliography

Administrative Office for a Continuing Presbyterian Church. "Minutes of the Advisory Convention of the Continuing Presbyterian Church." August 7–9, 1973. https://www.pcahistory.org/pca/ga/advisory_convention.pdf.

African American Ministries. "About African American Ministries." https://aampca.org/about/.

———. "LDR." https://aampca.org/conference/#faqs.

Alexander, T. Desmond. *The City of God and the Goal of Creation*. Short Studies in Biblical Theology. Wheaton, IL: Crossway, 2018.

———. *From Paradise to the Promised Land: An Introduction to the Pentateuch*. Grand Rapids: Baker Academic, 2002.

Alpha & Omega Ministries. "RAAN and 'Feeling Safe' Worshipping with 'White People.'" https://www.youtube.com/watch?v=liG-1r14ZM4

Arnold, Noelle Witherspoon, et al. "Psychological Heuristics and Faculty of Color: Racial Battle Fatigue and Tenure/Promotion." *Journal of Higher Education* 87.6 (2016) 890–919.

Auerbach, Carl, and Louise B. Silverstein. *Qualitative Data: An Introduction to Coding and Analysis*. New York: New York University Press, 2003.

Banks, Adelle M. "Church Confronts, Expels Member for Racist Views." *The Huffington Post* (August 4, 2010). http://www.huffingtonpost.com/2010/08/04/church-confronts-expels-m_n_671083.html.

Bavinck, Herman. "The Catholicity of Christianity and the Church." Translated by John Bolt. *Calvin Theological Journal* 27 (1992) 220–51.

———. *The Christian Family*. Translated by Nelson D. Kloosterman. Grand Rapids: Christian's Library, 2012.

———. "Common Grace." Translated by Raymond C. Van Leeuwen. *Calvin Theological Journal* 24 (1989) 35–65.

———. *Essays on Religion, Science, and Society*. Edited by John Bolt. Grand Rapids: Baker Academic, 2008.

———. "The Kingdom of God, the Highest Good." Translated by Nelson D. Kloosterman. *Bavinck Review* 2 (2011) 133–70.

———. *Our Reasonable Faith*. Grand Rapids: Eerdmans, 1956.

———. *The Philosophy of Revelation.* Ancaster, ON: Alev, 2012.

———. *Reformed Dogmatics: Abridged in One Volume.* Edited by John Bolt. Grand Rapids: Baker Academic, 2011.

———. *Reformed Dogmatics: God and Creation.* Edited by John Bolt. Translated by John Vriend. Grand Rapids: Baker Academic, 2004.

———. *Reformed Dogmatics: Holy Spirit, Church, and New Creation.* Edited by John Bolt. Translated by John Vriend. Grand Rapids: Baker Academic, 2008.

———. *Reformed Dogmatics: Prolegomena.* Edited by John Bolt. Translated by John Vriend. Grand Rapids: Baker Academic, 2003.

———. *Reformed Dogmatics: Sin and Salvation in Christ.* Edited by John Bolt. Translated by John Vriend. Grand Rapids: Baker Academic, 2006.

Berkhof, Louis. *Systematic Theology.* Grand Rapids: Eerdmans, 1996.

Berkouwer, G. C. *The Church.* Studies in Dogmatics. Grand Rapids.: Eerdmans, 1976.

———. *Man: The Image of God.* Studies in Dogmatics. Grand Rapids: Eerdmans, 1962.

———. *The Return of Christ.* Studies in Dogmatics. Grand Rapids: Eerdmans, 1972.

Blackburn, W. Ross. *The God Who Makes Himself Known: The Missionary Heart of the Book of Exodus.* Edited by Donald A. Carson. Downers Grove, IL: IVP Academic, 2012.

du Bois, W. E. B. *The Souls of Black Folk.* New York: Dover, 1994.

Bolt, John. "Editor's Introduction." In *Reformed Dogmatics: Prolegomena,* by Herman Bavinck, edited by John Bolt, translated by John Vriend, 11–22. Grand Rapids: Baker Academic, 2003.

Book of Common Prayer. New York: Church, 1979.

Bradley, Anthony B., ed. *Aliens in the Promised Land: Why Minority Leadership Is Overlooked in White Christian Churches and Institutions.* Phillipsburg, NJ: P&R, 2013.

———, ed. *Why Black Lives Matter: African American Thriving for the Twenty-First Century.* Eugene, OR: Cascade, 2020.

Bruner, Frederick Dale. *The Gospel of John: A Commentary.* Grand Rapids: Eerdmans, 2012.

Buice, Josh, et al. "The Statement on Social Justice & the Gospel." https://statementonsocialjustice.com/.

Calvin, John. *Galations.* 500th Anniversary Edition. Vol. 21 of *Calvin's Commentaries.* 23 vols. Grand Rapids: Baker, 2009.

———. *Genesis.* 500th Anniversary Edition. Vol. 1 of *Calvin's Commentaries.* 23 vols. Grand Rapids: Baker, 2009.

———. *Harmony of Exodus, Leviticus, Numbers, and Deuteronomy.* 500th Anniversary Edition. Vol. 2 of *Calvin's Commentaries.* 23 vols. Grand Rapids: Baker, 2009.

Carter, J. Kameron. *Race: A Theological Account.* New York: Oxford University Press, 2008.

Charles, Mark. "10 Reasons Why I'm Switching from Using the Term 'Racial Reconciliation' to Using the Term 'Racial Conciliation.'" *Wirelesshogan* (December 2, 2015). http://wirelesshogan.blogspot.com/2015/12/racial-conciliation.html.

Childs, Brevard S. *The Book of Exodus.* Louisville: Westminster John Knox, 1974.

Clowney, Edmund P. *The Church.* Downers Grove, IL: InterVarsity, 1995.

Committee on Mission to North America. "Pastoral Letter on Racism." https://pcahistory.org/topical/race/2004_pastoral_letter_on_racism.pdf.

Creswell, John W., and Cheryl N. Poth. *Qualitative Inquiry and Research Design: Choosing among Five Approaches.* Fourth ed. Los Angeles: SAGE, 2017.

Delitzsch, Franz. *A New Commentary on Genesis.* Vol. 1. 2 vols. Eugene, OR: Wipf & Stock, 2001.

———. *Isaiah.* Vol. 7 of *Keil & Delitzsch Commentary on the Old Testament.* 10 vols. Peabody, MA: Hendrickson, 2006.

DeYoung, Kevin. "Reparations: A Critical Theological Review." *The Gospel Coalition (Blog),* (April 22, 2021). https://www.thegospelcoalition.org/blogs/kevin-deyoung/reparations-a-critical-theological-review/.

Dixhoorn, Chad B., Van. *Confessing the Faith: A Reader's Guide to the Westminster Confession of Faith.* London: Banner of Truth Trust, 2016.

Dupont, Carolyn. "Jim Crow, Civil Rights, and Southern White Evangelicals: A Historians' Forum (Carolyn Dupont)." *The Gospel Coalition* (February 10, 2015). https://www.thegospelcoalition.org/blogs/justin-taylor/jim-crow-civil-rights-and-southern-white-evangelicals-a-historians-forum-carolyn-dupont/.

———. *Mississippi Praying: Southern White Evangelicals and the Civil Rights Movement, 1945–1975.* New York: New York University Press, 2013.

Duriez, Colin. *Francis Schaeffer: An Authentic Life.* Wheaton, IL: Crossway, 2008.

Eglinton, James. *Trinity and Organism: Towards a New Reading of Herman Bavinck's Organic Motif.* New York: T. & T. Clark, 2014.

Ellis, Carl F., Jr. *Free at Last?: The Gospel in the African-American Experience.* Downers Grove, IL: IVP Books, 1996.

———. "Reflections on Black Lives." *Prophets of Culture* (July 16, 2016). http://drcarlellisjr.blogspot.com/2016/07/reflections-on-black-lives.html.

Equal Justice Initiative. *Lynching in America: Confronting the Legacy of Racial Terror.* 3rd ed. Montgomery, AL: Equal Justice Initiative, 2017.

Evans, William, et al. "Critical Theory and the Unity of the Church." *The Ecclesial Calvinist* (August 31, 2017). https://theecclesialcalvinist.wordpress.com/2017/08/31/critical-theory-and-the-unity-of-the-church/.

Faulkner, William. *Requiem for a Nun.* Reprint edition. New York: Vintage, 2012.

Fensham, Charles. *The Books of Ezra and Nehemiah.* New International Commentary on the Old Testament. Grand Rapids: Eerdmans, 1983.

Fikse, Susan. "Diversity for the Sake of the Gospel." *byFaith* (April 4, 2016). http://byfaithonline.com/seeking-diversity-for-the-sake-of-the-gospel/.

Foley, Malcolm, and Justin Hawkins. "An Evangelical Response to the Statement on Social Justice & the Gospel." *Mere Orthodoxy* (September 27, 2018). https://mereorthodoxy.com/an-evangelical-response-to-the-statement-on-social-justice-and-the-gospel/.

Foulkes, Francis. *Ephesians: An Introduction and Commentary.* Tyndale New Testament Commentaries. Downers Grove, IL: IVP Academic, 1989.

Fowler, Megan. "The Diversity Dance." *byFaith* (July 11, 2016). http://byfaithonline.com/the-diversity-dance/.

France, R. T. *Matthew: An Introduction and Commentary.* Tyndale New Testament Commentaries. Downers Grove, IL: IVP Academic, 2008.

Geldenhuys, Norval. *Commentary on the Gospel of Luke.* New International Commentary on the New Testament. Grand Rapids: Eerdmans, 1971.

Green, Jay D. "New City Fellowship Chattanooga, Tennessee." *Reformed Journal* (June 1, 2010). http://reformedjournal.org/blog/2010/06/01/new-city-fellowship-chattanooga-tennessee/.

Hart, Drew G. I. *Trouble I've Seen: Changing the Way the Church Views Racism*. Harrisonburg, VA: Herald, 2016.

Hartley, John E. "Holy and Holiness, Clean and Unclean." In *Dictionary of the Old Testament: Pentateuch*, edited by T. Desmond Alexander, 420–29. Downers Grove, IL: IVP Academic, 2003.

Haynes, Stephen R. *The Last Segregated Hour: The Memphis Kneel-Ins and the Campaign for Southern Church Desegregation*. 1st ed. New York: Oxford University Press, 2012.

Hays, J. Daniel. *From Every People and Nation: A Biblical Theology of Race*. New Studies in Biblical Theology 14. Downers Grove, IL: IVP Academic, 2003.

Henry, Mickey. "PCA Repents for Failure to Demand Onesimus' Freedom." *Tribal Theocrat* (June 18, 2015). http://tribaltheocrat.com/2015/06/pca-repents-for-failure-to-demand-onesimus-freedom/.

Higgins, Michael. "African American Church Planters in the Presbyterian Church in America." DMin diss., Covenant Theological Seminary, 2012.

Hoekema, Anthony A. *The Bible and the Future*. Grand Rapids: Eerdmans, 1994.

Hudson, Darrell L., et al. "Racial Discrimination, John Henryism, and Depression among African Americans." *Journal of Black Psychology* 42.3 (2016) 221–43.

Ince, Irwyn L. *The Beautiful Community: Unity, Diversity, and the Church at its Best*. Downers Grove, IL: IVP, 2020.

"Interview on 'Meet the Press.'" *The Martin Luther King, Jr. Research and Education Institute* (April 17, 1960). https://kinginstitute.stanford.edu/king-papers/documents/interview-meet-press.

Jennings, Willie James. *The Christian Imagination: Theology and the Origins of Race*. New Haven: Yale University Press, 2011.

Johnson, Dennis E. *The Message of Acts in the History of Redemption*. Phillipsburg, NJ: P&R, 1997.

Johnson, Luke Timothy. *The Acts of the Apostles*. Sacra Pagina. Collegeville, MN: Glazier, 2006.

Joustra, Jessica. "An Embodied *Imago Dei*: How Herman Bavinck's Understanding of the Image of God Can Help Inform Conversations on Race." *Journal of Reformed Theology* 11 (2017) 9–23.

Katz, Andrew. "Unrest in Virginia." *TIME.com*, August 2017. https://time.com/charlottesville-white-nationalist-rally-clashes/.

Keil, C.F. *The Pentateuch*. Vol. 1 of *Commentary on the Old Testament*. 10 vols. Peabody, MA: Hendrickson, 2006.

Kidner, Derek. *Genesis*. Tyndale Old Testament Commentaries. Downers Grove, IL: IVP Academic, 2008.

King, Martin Luther, Jr. *The Words of Martin Luther King, Jr.* Selected by Coretta Scott King. New York: Newmarket, 1983.

Köhler, Ludwig, et al. *The Hebrew and Aramaic Lexicon of the Old Testament*. 5 vols. New York: Brill, 1994–2000.

Kruger, Melissa. "Looking Over the Fence." *TableTalk* (Septmber 10, 2017). https://www.ligonier.org/learn/devotionals/looking-over-the-fence.

Kruse, Colin G. *John: An Introduction and Commentary*. Tyndale New Testament Commentaries. Downers Grove, IL: IVP Academic, 2008.

Kwon, Duke. "Denominational Diversity and Cultural Normativity." *Scott Sauls (Blog)* (June 29, 2016). http://scottsauls.com/blog/2016/06/29/denominational-diversity-and-cultural-normativity/.

———. "Should We Abandon the Language of 'Racial Reconciliation?'" *The Gospel Coalition* (October 3, 2017). https://www.thegospelcoalition.org/article/should-we-abandon-the-language-of-racial-reconciliation/.

Kwon, Duke. and Gregory Thompson. *Reparations: A Christian Call for Repentance and Repair*. Grand Rapids: Brazos, 2021.

Lane, William L. *The Gospel According to Mark*. New International Commentary on the New Testament. Grand Rapids: Eerdmans, 1974.

LeCroy, Timothy R. "The [GA] Protest of 2015." *byFaith* (June 18 2015). http://byfaithonline.com/the-ga-protest-of-2015/.

———. "Transcript of Rev. Jim Baird's Speech." *Vita Pastoralis* (June 26, 2015). https://pastortimlecroy.wordpress.com/2015/06/16/transcript-of-rev-jim-bairds-speech/.

Lee, Morgen, and Caleb Lindgren. "John MacArthur's 'Statement on Social Justice' Is Aggravating Evangelicals," *Christianity Today* (September 12, 2018). https://www.christianitytoday.com/ct/podcasts/quick-to-listen/john-macarthur-statement-social-justice-gospel-thabiti.html/

Letham, Robert. *The Westminster Assembly: Reading Its Theology in Historical Context*. Phillipsburg, NJ: P&R, 2009.

Levering, Matthew. *Ezra & Nehemiah*. Brazos Theological Commentary on the Bible. Grand Rapids: Brazos, 2007.

Lewis, Lance. "Black Pastoral Leadership and Church Planting." In *Aliens in the Promised Land: Why Minority Leadership Is Overlooked in White Christian Churches and Institutions*, edited by Anthony B. Bradley, 29–43. Phillipsburg, NJ: P&R, 2013.

Lipka, Michael. "The Most and Least Racially Diverse U.S. Religious Groups. *Pew Research Center* (July 27, 2015). https://www.pewresearch.org/fact-tank/2015/07/27/the-most-and-least-racially-diverse-u-s-religious-groups/.

Livermore, David. *Cultural Intelligence: Improving Your CQ to Engage Our Multicultural World*. Grand Rapids: Baker, 2009.

Lucas, Sean Michael. *For a Continuing Church: The Roots of the Presbyterian Church in America*. Phillipsburg, NJ: P&R, 2015.

———. "Lost Legacies: African American Fathers and Brothers in Presbyterian History." Presented at the PCA General Assembly, Greensboro, NC, June 13, 2017.

———. *On Being Presbyterian: Our Beliefs, Practices, and Stories*. Phillipsburg, NJ: P&R, 2006.

———. *Robert Lewis Dabney: A Southern Presbyterian Life*. Phillipsburg, NJ: P&R, 2005.

Lucas, Sean Michael, and J. Ligon Duncan. "Personal Resolution on Civil Rights Remembrance." *byFaith* (June 10, 2015). http://byfaithonline.com/personal-resolution-on-civil-rights-remembrance/.

Lynching in America: Confronting the Legacy of Racial Terror. 3rd ed. Montgomery, AL: Equal Justice Initiative, 2017.

Marshall, I. Howard. *Acts: An Introduction and Commentary*. Tyndale New Testament Commentaries. Downers Grove, IL: IVP Academic, 2008.

McCaulley, Esau. *Reading While Black: African American Biblical Interpretation as an Exercise in Hope*. Downers Grove, IL: IVP Academic, 2020.

McKnight, Scot. *Galatians*. NIV Application Commentary. Grand Rapids: Zondervan, 1995.

———. *The Letter to Philemon*. Grand Rapids: Eerdmans, 2017.

Moore, Joy Jittaun. "Race." In *Dictionary of Scripture and Ethics*, edited by Joel B. Green et al., 653–55. Grand Rapids: Baker Academic, 2011.

Morris, Leon L. *Luke: An Introduction and Commentary*. Tyndale New Testament Commentaries. Downers Grove, IL: IVP Academic, 2008.

Motyer, J. Alec. *The Prophecy of Isaiah: An Introduction & Commentary*. Downers Grove, IL: InterVarsity, 1993.

National Presbyterian Church. "A Message to All Churches of Jesus Christ Throughout the World." Clinton, MS: Office of the Stated Clerk, 1973.

PCA Historical Center. "The Adopting Act of 1729." https://www.pcahistory.org/documents/subscription/adoptingact.html

PCA Mission to North America. "History of African American Presbyterianism." https://pcamna.org/wp-content/uploads/2018/06/AA-Timeline.pdf.

Plantinga, Cornelius, Jr. *Not the Way It's Supposed to Be: A Breviary of Sin*. Grand Rapids: Eerdmans, 1996.

Plummer, Wy. "Introducing the African American Presbyterian Fellowship." http://myemail.constantcontact.com/Introducing-the-African-American-Presbyterian-Fellowship.html?soid=1011275404028&aid=UL9sCsAL77c.

P&R News. "Assembly Adopts Racial Reconciliation Overture." *Presbyterian and Reformed News* 8.3 (September 2002) 4.

———. "Assembly Goes on Record as Being Opposed to Women in Combat." *Presbyterian and Reformed News* 8.3 (September 2002) 6.

———. "Assembly Refuses to Receive Personal Resolution in Opposition to League of the South." *Presbyterian and Reformed News* 8.3 (September 2002) 5.

———. "Interview with Morton Smith." *Presbyterian and Reformed News* 8.3 (September 2002) 14–15, 19.

Presbyterian Church in America. *Book of Church Order*. Lawrenceville, GA: Office of the Stated Clerk, 2021.

———. "Racial Reconciliation (2002)." https://pcahistory.org/topical/race/2002_racial_reconciliation.pdf.

———. "Report of the Ad Interim Committee on Racial and Ethnic Reconciliation to the Forty-Sixth General Assembly of the Presbyterian Church in America." https://www.mtw.org/CONTENT/About/Diversity/2018_PCAInterimReport_RacialReconciliation.pdf.

Ratzinger, Joseph Cardinal. '*In the Beginning . . .*': *A Catholic Understanding of the Story of Creation and the Fall*. Translated by Boniface Ramsey. Grand Rapids: Eerdmans, 1995.

Reconciliation and Justice Network. "About." http://www.reconciliationjusticenetwork.com/about/

Reformed Presbyterian Church, Evangelical Synod. "Report on Racial Questions." https://www.pcahistory.org/topical/race/1966_racial_questions.html.

Rhodes, C. J., and Jemar Tisby. "Black Ministers Release Charlottesville Declaration." *Clarion Ledger* (August 25, 2017). https://www.clarionledger.com/story/magnolia/faith/2017/08/25/black-ministers-release-charlottesville-declaration/601309001.

Robertson, Campbell. "A Quiet Exodus: Why Black Worshipers Are Leaving White Evangelical Churches." *The New York Times* (March 9, 2018). https://www.nytimes.com/2018/03/09/us/blacks-evangelical-churches.html.

Sarna, Nahum M. *The JPS Torah Commentary: Exodus*. Philadelphia: The Jewish Publication Society, 1991.

Sechrest, Love L. "Racism." In *Dictionary of Scripture and Ethics*, edited by Joel B. Green et al., 655. Grand Rapids: Baker Academic, 2011.

Serven, Doug, et al. *Heal Us, Emmanuel: A Call for Racial Reconciliation, Representation, and Unity in the Church*. Oklahoma City: White Blackbird, 2016.

Slade, Peter. *Open Friendship in a Closed Society: Mission Mississippi and a Theology of Friendship*. New York: Oxford University Press, 2009.

Smith, James K. A. *You Are What You Love: The Spiritual Power of Habit*. Grand Rapids: Brazos, 2016.

Smith, Morton. "The Racial Problem Facing America." *Tribal Theocrat* (March 16, 2014). http://tribaltheocrat.com/2014/03/dr-morton-h-smith-the-racial-problem-facing-america/.

Smith, William A., et al. "Between Hope and Racial Battle Fatigue: African American Men and Race-Related Stress." *Journal of Black Masculinity*, 2.1 (2011) 35–58.

———. "Racial Battle Fatigue and the MisEducation of Black Men: Racial Microaggressions, Societal Problems, and Environmental Stress." *Journal of Negro Education* 80.1 (2011) 63–82.

Sparkman, Wayne. "History of PCA Motto: 'Faithful to the Scriptures, True to the Reformed Faith, and Obedient to the Great Commission.'" *The Aquila Report* (September 10, 2017). https://www.theaquilareport.com/history-pca-motto-faithful-scriptures-true-reformed-faith-obedient-great-commission/.

Spykman, Gordon J. *Reformational Theology: A New Paradigm for Doing Dogmatics*. Grand Rapids: Eerdmans, 1992.

Sue, Derald Wing. "Racial Microaggressions in Everyday Life: Is Subtle Bias Harmless?" *Psychology Today* (October 5, 2010). http://www.psychologytoday.com/blog/microaggressions-in-everyday-life/201010/racial-microaggressions-in-everyday-life.

Taylor, Kenneth. "The Spirituality of the Church: Segregation, The Presbyterian Journal, and the Origins of the Presbyterian Church in America, 1942–1973." *Reformed Perspectives* 9.34 (August 2007) 1–47. http://reformedperspectives.org/articles/ken_taylor/ken_taylor.church.spirituality.pdf.

Thompson, Gregory, and Duke Kwon. "Sanctifying the Status Quo: A Response to Kevin DeYoung." *The Front Porch* (July 19, 2021). https://thefrontporch.org/2021/07/sanctifying-the-status-quo-a-response-to-reverend-kevin-deyoung/.

Thompson, John L. *Genesis 1–11*. Reformation Commentary on Scripture. Downers Grove, IL: IVP Academic, 2012.

Tisby, Jemar. "The Downside of Integration for Black Christians." *The Witness* (August 21, 2017). https://thewitnessbcc.com/downside-integration-black-christians/.

———. "An Indigenous Reformed Movement in African American Communities." *The Witness BCC* (June 16, 2014). https://thewitnessbcc.com/indigenous-reformed-movement-african-american-communities.

———. "The Journey from RAAN to 'The Witness: A Black Christian Collective.'" *The Witness* (October 31, 2017). https://thewitnessbcc.com/raan-witness-black-christian-collective/.

———. "Know Your Black Presbyterians, Pt. 1: The Pioneers." *The Witness* (June 17, 2015). https://thewitnessbcc.com/know-your-black-presbyterians-pt-1-the-pioneers/.

———. "Trump's Election and Feeling 'Safe' in White Evangelical Churches." *The Witness* (November 18, 2016). https://thewitnessbcc.com/trumps-election-feeling-safe-white-evangelical-churches/.

Tisby, Jemar, and Tyler Burns. "Processing Donald Trump with Jemar Tisby." Produced by Beau York and Lean More. *Pass the Mic*, November 10, 2016. Podcast, 44:17. https://podcasts.apple.com/us/podcast/pass-the-mic/id1435500798?i=1000419238560.

Veenhof, Jan. *Nature and Grace in Herman Bavinck*. Translated by Albert M. Wolters. Sioux Center, IA: Dordt College Press, 2006.

Volf, Miroslav. *Exclusion & Embrace: A Theological Exploration of Identity, Otherness, and Reconciliation*. Nashville: Abingdon, 1996.

Waltke, Bruce K., and Cathi J. Fredricks. *Genesis: A Commentary*. Grand Rapids: Zondervan, 2001.

Webb, Andrew. "An Open Reply to Jemar Tisby and 'The Downside of Integration for Black Christians.'" *Building Old School Churches* (August 23, 2017). https://biblebased.wordpress.com/2017/08/22/an-open-reply-to-jemar-tisby-and-the-downside-of-integration-for-black-christians/.

Westminster Confession of Faith. Lawrenceville, GA: Committee on Discipleship Ministries, 2005.

Whitfield, Russ. "Ferguson and Your Local Church: A Plea for Building Cross-Cultural Community (Pt. 1)." *Grace DC Church Network* (August 21, 2014). https://downtown.gracedc.net/latest/blog/ferguson-and-your-local-church-part-1.

Wilkerson, Isabel. *The Warmth of Other Suns: The Epic Story of America's Great Migration*. Reprint ed. New York: Vintage, 2011.

Williams, Ronald J. *Williams' Hebrew Syntax*. Edited by John C. Beckman. 3rd ed. Toronto: University of Toronto Press, 2007.

Williamson, H. G. M. *Ezra, Nehemiah*. Edited by David Allen Hubbard and Glenn W. Barker. Vol. 16 of *Word Biblical Commentary*. 61 vols. Grand Rapids: Zondervan, 2015.

Wilson, Joseph M. *The Presbyterian Historical Almanac and Annual Remembrancer of the Church for 1863*. Philadelphia: Wilson, 1863.

Wilson, Wendy. "Conservative Presbyterian Seminary in St. Louis to Hold Conference Featuring Leftist Teachings on Race." *Tennessee Star* (August 30, 2017). http://tennesseestar.com/2017/08/30/conservative-presbyterian-seminary-in-st-louis-to-hold-conference-featuring-leftist-teachings-on-race/.

Wolters, Albert M. *Creation Regained: Biblical Basics for a Reformational Worldview*. 2nd ed. Grand Rapids: Eerdmans, 2005.

Wright, N. T. *Colossians and Philemon*. Downers Grove, IL: IVP Academic, 2008.

———. *Paul and the Faithfulness of God*. 2 vols. Minneapolis: Fortress, 2013.

Yancey, George. *Beyond Racial Gridlock: Embracing Mutual Responsibility*. Westmont, IL: InterVarsity, 2009.

Yosso, Tara J., et al. "Critical Race Theory, Racial Microaggressions, and Campus Climate for Latino/A Undergraduates." *Harvard Educational Review* 79.4 (2009) 659–90.